FRANKIE DETTORI

The Illustrated Biography

Also by John Karter

LESTER: RETURN OF A LEGEND

FRANKIE DETTORI
The Illustrated Biography

John Karter

HEADLINE

First published in 1995
by HEADLINE BOOK PUBLISHING

10 9 8 7 6 5 4 3 2 1

British Library Cataloguing in Publication Data

Karter, John
Frankie Dettori
I. Title
798.40092

ISBN 0-7472-1659-2 (hardback)
0-7472-7777-X (softback)

Designed by Clive Dorman
Typeset from author's disks & b/w origination by Clive Dorman & Co.
Colour origination by P&W Graphics PTE LTD Singapore

Printed and bound in Great Britain by
Butler & Tanner Ltd, Frome

HEADLINE BOOK PUBLISHING
A division of Hodder Headline PLC
338 Euston Road
London NW1 3BH

To Jack Kennedy. Thanks for the memories.

Picture Credits

CONTENTS

Acknowledgements

I am extremely grateful to so many people without whose help this book would not have been possible. Many thanks to all of you, in particular Luca Cumani, Ian Balding, Gerald Leigh, John Gosden, Ray Cochrane, Giorgio Barsotti, Cliff Woof and Alan Byrne.

PREFACE

Frankie Dettori is the best thing to have happened to racing for years. That is not a personal accolade (although I certainly would not disagree with the sentiment), but a tribute that cropped up time and again as I talked to racing folk across the spectrum during my researches into the story of this remarkable young man's life.

'Come on Frankie!' – the call rings out like a mantra in betting shops and at the track in the way they used to bay for Lester Piggott in his heyday. Having Dettori on your horse, whether it happens to be in the glitter of Royal Ascot and Longchamp or the more mundane cut and thrust of Catterick and Chepstow, is a source of joy and inspiration for racing professionals, punters and once-a-year dabblers alike.

The fanaticism for Frankie has evolved not merely because he has proved himself arguably the most complete rider since Piggott, but because he does what he does with such flair and obvious enjoyment. The charismatic young Italian transcends the sport of kings in a way that no other individual has done since Piggott.

Dettori's natural showmanship has cut a swathe through the strait-laced insularity of the racing world. With his exuberance and his all-consuming passion for racing and life, he somehow always manages to take centre stage whether he is riding to victory on one of Sheikh Mohammed's pricey thoroughbreds, leaping theatrically from his mount in the winner's enclosure, or eliciting a rare smile from the Sheikh with a display of hugs and kisses that no one else could get away with.

As to his ability in the saddle, his natural horsemanship, allied to the distinctive crouch and the fine sense of pace which he learnt in successive winters in the United States, have combined to make him a consummate rider and brought him a richly deserved first championship at the age of 24.

If that all sounds a bit sugary, well, so be it. Judging by the many different people I spoke to within the game, it would be nigh on impossible to find anyone with anything seriously negative to say about Frankie Dettori.

Sure, Frankie did a few brash things in his youth, but who hasn't? And now that he has matured into the complete professional in every way it seems there is nothing to stop him dominating the championship for the next ten years or more. I, and many thousands of others, look forward to that prospect immensely.

CHAPTER ONE
FRANKIE GOES TO HOLLYWOOD

Luca Cumani, Derby-winning trainer and plunderer of many of racing's most prestigious international prizes, stood in the heady glare of the winner's circle at Churchill Downs in Kentucky and felt the tears welling up inside him. Cumani, whose patrons over the years had included such luminaries of the turf as the Aga Khan and Sheikh Mohammed, had experienced many of the highs and a few of the desperate lows of the racing game, but never in his life had he felt a surge of emotion quite like this.

There in front of him, walking proudly into that coveted enclosure, garlanded with the traditional blanket of purple and gold chrysanthemums presented to winners of racing's $10 million dollar series, the Breeders' Cup, was his handsome bay colt, Barathea, a horse that had provided him with some of the best but also some of the most frustrating moments of his career.

In Cumani's justifiable opinion, Barathea would have gone down as the best miler of the decade had fortune been just a little more on his side. Cumani, who is the son of the ten-times champion Italian trainer, Sergio, is a painstaking and patient strategist, and, putting behind him the crushing disappointments with Barathea, he had plotted one last throw of the dice that he believed might seal the horse's career with a monster success.

The towering triumph Barathea had just achieved over an international field in the 1994 Breeders' Cup Mile on a golden autumn afternoon had been planned with military precision. Yet now that the dream had become a glorious reality it was almost too much for him to take in.

As Cumani felt his cheeks grow moist with a feeling of rapture that almost transcended his Derby victory with Kahyasi six years previously, the real source of his joy was the pencil-slim figure on Barathea's back, his brilliant but occasionally infuriating young countryman, Lanfranco 'Frankie' Dettori.

Bouncing back from the devastation of his crushing defeat aboard the European speed queen, Lochsong, earlier in the afternoon, Dettori had just ridden the perfect race to bring Barathea home clear of his field with the style and panache that brought him his first jockeys' championship that year at the age of 24. As Dettori jumped from Barathea's back with the kind of flamboyant leap made famous by the great Angel Cordero, Cumani was filled not just with a deep sense of professional gratification but also with a kind of glowing

Leap of faith: Dettori executes a flying dismount from Barathea after winning the Breeders'
Cup Mile in Kentucky, a victory that climaxed his reunion with Barathea's trainer Luca
Cumani (left).

paternal pride as well.

In many ways their story was like the homecoming of the Prodigal. Cumani
had taken Dettori under his wing since the time Frankie, then aged fourteen
and a half, arrived in Britain nine years previously shivering with cold and
unable to speak a word of English. Sent over by his father, Gianfranco,
thirteen-times champion jockey of Italy, to pursue his dream of being a jockey
in the more rarefied atmosphere of the British circuit, young Frankie very
quickly found himself homesick and demoralised.

That he did not turn tail and scurry back to his homeland was due in great
part to Cumani's support and guidance. Cumani has a son and daughter of his
own, but with Frankie so far away from the father he idolised, Cumani and his
wife, Sara, took it upon themselves to treat Frankie as one of the family.

Instantly taken by Dettori's appealing character, Cumani spent far more time with his young protégé than he would normally do with any other apprentice rider in his yard.

Cumani does not dismiss the suggestion that Dettori became like a son to him. 'Yes, I have quite a bit of affection for Frankie,' he says with what is almost certainly a degree of understatement. Despite his closeness to his own father, Dettori appeared to reciprocate that affection.

Cumani had also demonstrated the most remarkable faith in Dettori's ability when he took what appeared to be a major gamble in elevating him to the position of number one rider for his high-profile Newmarket yard at the age of 18 when Ray Cochrane left to go elsewhere.

It seemed all the more incomprehensible and bizarre, therefore, when Dettori suddenly turned his back on Cumani, and the security of a job that offered both status and a platform from which to launch a challenge for the jockeys' title, in order to pursue transitory fame and fortune in Hong Kong.

As we shall see in more detail later, Cumani was both stunned and deeply saddened by Dettori's behaviour and so, acting in the role of a punitive father, purely for Dettori's own good, he temporarily severed all ties with him and basically told him to rethink his whole attitude and grow up.

In a twist that seemingly left him out in the cold in terms of a principal retainer, Dettori forfeited his Hong Kong contract as a result of a brush with the law over an alleged drugs incident. But, having appeared likely to be left struggling as a freelance, he maintained his incredible propensity for being in the right place at the right time by securing a contract to ride for the world's most powerful owner, Sheikh Mohammed, whose racing colours he wore aboard Barathea.

Having put himself back on course to fulfil his cherished aim of becoming champion jockey, Dettori then sought an emotional reconciliation with Cumani a few months later. Seeing Dettori was genuinely contrite, Cumani was only too pleased to forgive and forget – with one notable exception. Sticking to his word, Cumani refused to give Dettori the mount on any of his horses for a whole year.

So it was that just over twelve months after the two men buried their differences the old firm got together once more – again in fortuitous circumstances for Dettori – to bring off what many were beginning to believe was verging on the impossible. Britain had managed only two successes in the ten previous runnings of the Breeders' Cup, but now the army of British racing fans who had travelled over to Kentucky and the thousands watching back home in the United Kingdom on the closed-circuit satellite feed were cheering frenetically for a stunning British success brought about by two Italians and an Arab Sheikh.

As the backslapping and the well-wishing seemed to go on forever, Cumani,

15

and indeed Barathea, would have conceded that there was no doubt who was the star of this very special racing show. As Dettori sat motionless on Barathea waiting to unleash that final surge of power while all around him jockeys flailed away to no avail, the frantic cries of 'Come on, Frankie!' were not borne solely out of patriotic or even financial considerations.

With his unquenchable smile and spontaneous displays of unbridled joy, Dettori had become the favourite son of a whole nation of racing enthusiasts, who had arguably not taken anyone to their hearts so closely since Lester Piggott in his heyday. At the end of the year Dettori would finish with 233 British victories, the highest total since Sir Gordon Richards was amassing his huge scores in the 1940s; but while Dettori's ability in the saddle was already being acclaimed as the best since Lester, statistics on this occasion were almost irrelevant.

As Dettori took off through the air with the theatrical Cordero leap that was to appear on the pages of countless newspapers and other publications, it represented an incredible climax to the burgeoning love affair between the

Luca Cumani and his wife Sara greet their 1988 Derby winner Kahyasi. The couple treated Dettori as one of the family when he came to England from Italy and Luca was almost like a second father to him.

young Italian and his adoring public. It was a triumph so compelling and captivating in its execution and its showmanship that only Dettori could have carried it off.

For the misty-eyed Cumani the victory of Dettori and Barathea was many things rolled into one. Professional satisfaction, personal fulfilment and sheer primitive excitement all contributed to his state of elation as he surveyed the euphoric scene beneath the famous twin spires of Churchill Downs. Above all, though, it was about having Dettori back in harness for an occasion that was unique even in his vast experience of the wonderful, topsy-turvy business of horse racing.

Cumani admits that nothing could ever surpass his Derby victory with Kahyasi, but in another sense he regards the Breeders' Cup as matchless. 'The Derby is the Derby and nothing can equal it,' Cumani says. 'But in terms of pure emotion the Breeders' Cup was the best thing that will ever happen to me until I win the Derby with Frankie up.'

Having regained much of his former high standing in the training ranks following a period when circumstances conspired to force him down the league table, Cumani's dream may not be too fanciful. The best is certainly yet to come from Dettori, who could easily enjoy another two decades at the top. As Cumani says: 'If he continues in this vein he'll go down as one of the best of all time.'

As the Milanese marvel thrusts onwards and upwards towards heady new horizons, even Lester and the great Sir Gordon could be in danger of eclipse. In professional and personal terms, British racing has never seen anything quite like the irrepressible ray of Italian sunshine named Frankie Dettori.

The prospect of such mega-stardom would have seemed about as likely as Dettori becoming President of Italy when he first became involved in racing in a serious way. He once admitted that he had a habit of falling off in his early days in Italy, and Cumani remembers him being more on the ground than in the saddle.

'When Frankie first came to me he was not very good. He was very weak and small and he used to fall off every day,' Cumani says. 'I remember in particular he used to ride a horse of mine called Dallas, who won the Cambridgeshire. The old horse used to drop him every day and stand there looking down at him, while Frankie lay there feeling sorry for himself.'

Cumani, who was a champion amateur rider before he turned to training, is adamant that being a jockey does not come naturally. 'Nobody is born a jockey,' he says. Even so, based on what he knew of Dettori's background, he must have been expecting just a touch more promise from the young man who arrived at his Bedford House stables on a bone-chilling day in the winter of 1985.

In one way, at least, the liaison between Luca Cumani and Frankie Dettori

Frankie's father, Gianfranco Dettori, is led in by owner Carlo d'Alessio after winning the 1976 2,000 Guineas on Wollow. He had won the race in 1975 on d'Alessio's horse Bolkonski, also trained by Henry Cecil.

might have seemed the most natural thing in the world. Gianfranco Dettori had ridden as first jockey for Sergio Cumani for many years when the two of them reigned supreme in Italian racing. Gianfranco, who had a deep admiration for the British racing scene, had spent a lot of time riding in the United Kingdom in the seventies, principally for the ten-times champion trainer, Henry Cecil, for whom he won the 2,000 Guineas on Bolkonski and Wollow in 1975 and 1976.

Gianfranco had considerable regrets about not having taken the opportunity to base himself in Britain permanently. So, when young Lanfranco made it clear that he wanted to become a jockey too, Dettori senior decided that it would not do for his son to remain in Italy where he would never find the kind of international success and standing he himself had never quite attained. Gianfranco was convinced that the only place for his son to go in order to make his way into the upper echelons of the racing world was Britain where the sport was on a different plane and the opportunities were altogether more widespread.

It appears that Gianfranco did not want his son to further his career in Italy for another, more practical, reason. Knowing the way some cynical minds worked, he felt that for him to ride against Frankie on a regular basis on the Italian circuit could lead to allegations of race fixing when they were in the same event and results did not go the way punters expected.

Gianfranco also wanted the best possible start in life for his beloved son because of his own background. He had come from a poor family in Serravana in Sardinia where the kind of luxuries he took for granted in his jet-setting life as a top jockey were mere fantasies. Struggling for every last lira had been a daily fact of life for Gianfranco and that was the last thing he wanted Lanfranco to do.

Gianfranco was the son of a bricklayer and he had four brothers – Sergio, who also teamed up with Sergio Cumani and is a leading rider in Italy with over 1,500 winners; Sandro and Guiseppe, who work in racing stables; and Salvatore, who still lives in Sardinia. Gianfranco, seeking his fortune away from the dead-end of life in Sardinia, travelled to Rome and found a job washing dishes in a restaurant, sleeping on the damp floor of a cellar.

Gianfranco then went to work in a market where fate stepped in to shape his life and ultimately Frankie's too. The owner of the stall, a policeman, had connections in the trotting world and helped the diminutive Gianfranco obtain the offer of a job working with trotters at the Tor di Valle track in Rome, which he took with no hesitation despite the fact that he received no wages.

Gianfranco did not see a racehorse until he was 18, when he obtained work as a stable lad in Rome, and he did not sit on one until he was 20. It was at that relatively advanced age that he rode his first winner in Milan. No one could have guessed then that he would top the jockeys' table a remarkable thirteen times.

An Italian without a little passion and romance in his soul would not be a true Italian, and soon after he had launched his racing career Gianfranco went to the circus, fell in love with the trapeze artist and married her. His high-flying bride was named Mara. She was 16 and Gianfranco was 21.

Almost inevitably the whirlwind romance eventually died and the couple broke up when Frankie was five. Their union had also produced a daughter, Alessandra, who is six years older than Frankie and now lives near Milan. At the time of the break-up Frankie went to live with his father and Alessandra went with her mother. Frankie is extremely fond of his sister and sees her as often as he can. She has two lovely children on whom uncle Frankie dotes, which might explain why he is frequently photographed holding babies with a look of complete confidence and enjoyment on his face.

Having a famous father can as often turn a child away from that particular way of life as attract him to it. There was no doubt in young Frankie's mind, however. He recalls being unmoved by his father's successive triumphs in the 2,000 Guineas, but he was only five at the time. Once the childhood fantasies

Pony express: Dettori, aged 10, on one of his first pony rides in Milan. His early experience of race riding was gained on the pony circuit, but, as his look of determination shows, he was keen to move swiftly into the more serious business of horse racing.

about being a petrol pump attendant had been quelled and he visited his first race meeting at the age of seven, he knew that he wanted to be a *fantino*, just like his father.

It was at that time that his father bought him a pony, which he kept in the garden of their villa in Milan. Frolicking around on his pony gave Dettori his first rudimentary riding skills, but he very soon came to realise that he wanted far more than a bit of gentle fun in his back yard. So when he was 10 or 11, he got himself involved in pony racing, which used to take place on the racetrack in Milan after the horse racing had finished.

Donning the red, white and green colours of Carlo d'Alessio, the Rome lawyer, whose colours Gianfranco had worn to victory in both 2,000 Guineas, young Frankie would give full rein to his imagination, picturing himself riding a finish against the best jockeys in the world in front of thousands of cheering fans.

The pony circuit was soon past its sell-by date in Frankie's eyes and, seeking out the real thing, he began accompanying his father to the stables of the Botti brothers, Alduino and Guiseppe, who, with some 200 horses at their stables in Milan and Rome, controlled the most powerful and successful training operation in Italy, winning the trainers' championship twenty-one years in a row.

Dettori was 12 when he first felt the addictive sensation of sitting astride a sleek thoroughbred with real gears. To the young lad used to cajoling stubborn ponies into action it was like switching from a tiny Fiat to a Ferrari. As we have seen he fell off quite a bit, but he learned a lot too, much of it coming in the guise of endless bouts of constructive criticism from his doting father.

Fathers teaching sons can be a recipe for disaster, but Gianfranco, who has remained a constant source of encouragement throughout Frankie's career – their phone calls to one another must have outnumbered those of the White House – was the best and most sympathetic coach Frankie could have had.

Dettori recalls that his father was alongside him when he had his very first canter, saying 'Do this, do that. Pull this, pull that,' while he hung on somewhat bemused like a learner driver who feels he simply doesn't have enough hands to cope.

As a precursor to the distinctive, streamlined style Dettori was to develop, principally through visits to the United States, his father also used to whack Frankie's bottom to make him keep it down. There were no parental whackings of a more serious type for failing to pursue his academic endeavours, only encouragement, and Dettori left his private college in Milan shortly before he was 14 to become an apprentice.

A few months later Dettori was to have the first meeting with the man who was to have the greatest influence on his life apart from his father. It took place at Pisa racecourse during the winter when Gianfranco introduced his son to Cumani and asked him if he would consider taking him on at his Newmarket yard.

Luca Matteo Cumani had first come to Britain in 1971 to work for John Winter, the Newmarket trainer, in his school holidays. He returned the following year to ride Meissen to victory in the Moët et Chandon Silver Magnum, the race known as the amateurs' Derby, showing the style and judgement that gained him 85 winners on the amateur circuit. In December 1973 he came over again to work for Henry Cecil and stayed on, taking out a licence in his own right just over two years later.

That's my boy: Frankie's father was an enormous source of help and encouragement to him throughout his early career. Their closeness is evident in this picture taken in Rome when Frankie was 16.

Cumani quickly established himself in the top flight, gaining a reputation as a man who was as accomplished at the difficult business of winning major prizes overseas as he was on the domestic front. An elegant man who commands respect, he is one of the most outspoken commentators on matters affecting his beloved sport of horse racing.

Cumani numbers victories in the Derby, Irish Derby, Italian Derby, St Leger (giving Lester Piggott a record twenty-eighth British classic win with Commanche Run in 1984), America's Arlington Million and Breeders' Cup Mile among his glittering collection of international prizes. His status in the 'sport of kings' was acknowledged by the Queen when he and his wife, Sara, rode in one of the carriages in the Royal Procession at Ascot in 1992. Despite his high standing, however, Cumani is not averse to a little self-mocking, frequently describing himself as 'a wop living in Britain'.

Cumani looks back fondly to that first meeting with the boy who was to take him for a ride on an emotional roller-coaster. 'I remember being introduced to Frankie by Gianfranco, who told me he was keen to send him over,' Cumani says. 'I didn't really form any lasting impressions of him at that stage except that he was very small – about this high [holding his hand at knee level] – and very cheeky. He arrived at my yard two weeks later, complaining about the cold. At that stage he was a bit of a runaway, a bit wild.'

Cumani's last remark does not refer to any delinquency on Dettori's part. What lay behind the apparent lack of self-discipline was the fact that, although his father was a great source of support as far as becoming a jockey went, the young Dettori lacked true parental guidance. Gianfranco, who had married again to a French woman named Christine, was away riding much of the time, so Frankie was left to work through the difficult transition to his teenage years largely on his own.

There was, however, one source of support from the beginning. Teresa Colangeli, the wife of the late trainer Vincenzo, knew Dettori literally from the very beginning and became like a second mother to him. When Frankie was born on 15 December 1970, his father was away riding in Australia and Teresa took his mother to the hospital to give birth. Neither of them could possibly have guessed that the tiny infant who was to lie screaming in Mara's arms hours later would not merely emulate his father, but become an international superstar.

When Gianfranco was away, which inevitably in a jockey's life means more often than not, Teresa stepped in to take care of the little lad she grew to love like a son. Frankie spent a lot of time living in her house in Verese and even now he keeps in constant touch with her, visiting her whenever he is riding in Italy and phoning her twice a week. When he rides a big winner she is the first person he phones to share his triumph with after his father.

For her part, Teresa has nothing but the greatest affection for Frankie, describing him as 'A very sweet child and a good kid.' She follows his career diligently and, as with almost everyone Dettori comes into contact with, she has nothing but good to say about him.

The teenager Cumani first encountered was a little more complex, however. Being packed off to Newmarket in the dead of winter with no knowledge of the language and very little money in his pocket had only compounded Dettori's growing pains. There he was at the epicentre of the finest racing in the world, having been given a heaven-sent opportunity to work for one of the country's leading trainers, yet he was not a happy young man. Setting out to be an Italian version of Lester Piggott was all very well, but the reality was very different from the fantasy.

'The first six months when I couldn't speak English were like prison,' he said. 'I was living in a very small room and it was work, bed, work, bed and nothing else. The weather was terrible, the food was strange and so were the people and I became very depressed.'

The lilting Cockney–Italian accent that Dettori developed probably had its origins in his move to a more spacious bed-sit when he aquired his first room-mate. The other lad, who also worked for Cumani, peppered his conversation with rhyming slang which, not surprisingly, left Dettori even more confused: 'He kept saying things like "Me old china – mate" and "Apples and pears –

stairs". I didn't have a clue what he was talking about!'

Constant reassuring phone calls from his father helped him to stay the course and things gradually got better as spring arrived and Newmarket emerged from its hibernation and began to buzz with the heady expectation of a new season. Andrea Pecoraro, who was the son of Rosario, a trainer for whom Dettori worked in Italy, had come over to work as assistant to Cumani and he offered Dettori a little moral support and a few pointers in English, although his command of the language was only a short head in front of Dettori's.

Young Frankie also picked up the language at Newmarket's New Astley Club, a meeting place for stable lads run by Ron Wallwork, a gold medal winner in the 20 kilometre walk at the 1966 Commonwealth Games. Every summer the lads from the club took part in a Donkey Derby held on the Jubilee recreation ground. There was betting on the race, but it was not taken too seriously as donkeys and riders went off in all directions.

Wallwork recalls: 'Frankie's first winner was in the Donkey Derby. He was a likeable lad with an infectious laugh and got on very well with the other lads. He was always game to try anything and he picked up a lot of his English here.'

Dettori soon found that the English were not quite as unfriendly as he had first thought. 'You English are not easy to get to know, but gradually I made friends,' he told me in an early interview.

Cumani, who was impressed enough by the young tearaway to offer him an indefinite extension of his six-months stay, does not remember him being constantly down in the dumps, quite the opposite. 'He was always very cheeky and very happy,' Cumani recalls. 'He might not have spoken a word of English when he arrived, but Frankie has never been one to be lost for words and he would still talk non-stop. Even though he was a bit wild, he always had something going for him.'

The cheekiness Cumani spoke of soon landed Dettori in hot water with the guvnor. 'When he first came he was mucking out and doing his two like any other lad,' Cumani says. 'When he turned 15 he occasionally rode a few horses at exercise. One of them was a horse called Saker, who ran promisingly first time out and then went for a race at York which he was expected to win.

'All the lads had backed Saker, but he got beaten. At evening stables Frankie said "The guvnor couldn't train ivy up a wall", or couldn't train a bicycle – something like that. When I heard about it I grabbed him, picked him up by his shirt and held him up against a wall. "Listen," I said, "maybe I can't train ivy up a wall, but to you I'm the greatest trainer in the world. Understand?"'

Putting on a look of mock terror, Cumani laughs as he recalls Dettori's reaction: 'Frankie just shook his head and went "Yes, yes, yes!". I think he got the message.'

Cumani's contention that jockeys are made, not born, helped him make an objective assessment of the little lad with the God-given talent for falling off when others might not have bothered. 'As soon as he started riding out seriously for me the following year I realised he had something that set him apart. But, at that stage I viewed him as a jockey with potential, no more than that. It was a case of how much he would improve,' Cumani says.

He was ready to race ride at 15, according to Cumani. However, under Jockey Club rules no one can hold a licence to ride in Britain until they are 16. So, during the British close season Dettori went back to Italy where there is no such restriction and gained the first victory of his career aboard Rif, trained by Alduino Botti, on 16 November 1986, at Turin.

Beaming as if he had won a Derby, an almost cherubic-looking Dettori was still a month short of his sixteenth birthday as he returned exultantly to the winner's enclosure. If following in his father's footsteps was Frankie's aim he wasn't doing too badly for starters. He had beaten him to that initial win by more than four years, and before he reached the age when Gianfranco rode his first winner Frankie would achieve the kind of success and recognition his father would never have dreamt possible for his son.

Bruce Raymond, a former leading jockey and now assistant racing manager to Sheikh Maktoum al Maktoum, remembers riding against Dettori in Italy. 'I got to know Frankie quite well when I was out there,' Raymond says. 'In Italy the jockeys are very much tied down by orders – "Do this and do that". But Frankie looked very special and out of the ordinary even then. You had to keep reminding yourself he was only 15. Most of the people he was riding against were far more experienced and that's still true today.'

During that winter in Italy, Dettori served two or three months with Antonio Verdicchio in Pisa. Verdicchio recalls that Dettori's dedication to the job shone through from the beginning. 'He was always very determined to be a jockey,' Verdicchio says. 'He took his job very seriously and never missed one morning riding out or carrying out his duties as a stable lad. He never ate very much because he was always watching his weight.'

Dettori stayed in Verdicchio's house and the trainer was very much taken with his personality as well as his professionalism. 'He was a brilliant guy. He had a very strong character, but was always very charming and made friends very easily,' Verdicchio says.

There were sixteen more winners on the board by the time Dettori returned to England for the beginning of the 1987 season. Cumani was now convinced that Dettori would make a jockey and was ready to let him off the leash and into the public arena in Britain. However, it was not Cumani but Peter Walwyn who gave Dettori his first taste of a British racecourse. Walwyn let himself in for a post-race exchange with young Frankie that was not quite what he expected.

Walwyn, twice champion trainer, landed his greatest triumph with Grundy in the 1975 Derby. He is a fascinating and extremely popular character. Very much the quintessential English gentleman, whose off-track pursuits are of the

hunting–shooting variety, this public-school educated son of an army officer is nevertheless down to earth and possessed of a great sense of fun.

Nicknamed Basil because of his resemblance in looks and demeanour to John Cleese's alter ego, Basil Fawlty, Walwyn can see humour in most situations. For example, Walwyn tells how, after he won the Derby with Grundy, he was driving from Epsom and had to make an emergency stop at a public toilet in Esher. He recalls: 'I saw this slogan written on the wall in front of me. It said "The future of Britain is in your hands". I love things like that. I still laugh about it now.'

Walwyn found it no laughing matter when Dettori came back into the unsaddling enclosure after that first ride in Britain. Having ridden those

OPPOSITE Here's looking at you kid: A baby-faced Dettori talks tactics with trainer Rosario Pecoraro and his son Stefano before a race in Livorno, Italy.

RIGHT Trainer Peter Walwyn, who gave Dettori his first mount in Britain. Walwyn found his noted sense of humour deserting him in a post-race exchange after the horse finished second.

winners in Italy, Dettori was entitled to claim only a 5lb allowance instead of 7lb, but that allowance and other factors led Walwyn to book the unknown Italian kid for a race at the Kempton Park Easter meeting in 1987.

'He rode a very good looking horse for me named Mustakbil, owned by Sheikh Hamdan al Maktoum,' Walwyn recalls. 'I wanted an apprentice to take the weight off the horse's back. I knew Frankie's father was a good jockey and they told me he was a very good little rider. Anyway, he finished second and when he got off the horse he patted its tummy and said " 'E run well, but 'e fet (*sic*)".

'I said "What do you mean?" and he said "He's fet".

'Suddenly I realised what he meant and I said "You cheeky little bugger – he's not fat!". I'll say one thing for Frankie, though, the horse never won a race.'

Despite the cheek, Walwyn formed a favourable impression of the lad with the mischievous brown eyes, who was still as slim as a piece of tagliatelle. 'He had a lot of style about him even then. You could sense he'd go a long way,' Walwyn says. 'He'd got that bit of devil about him, that bit of spark. They've got to have that to take their chances and go for gaps. Lester's got it and so has Pat [Eddery]. They've got to have a sizzle about them to get on and Frankie had it alright.'

There was no instant lift-off for Dettori, however: it was almost two months later before he posted his first victory in Britain. The breakthrough came at Goodwood in June aboard one of Cumani's horses, Lizzy Hare, named after his secretary. It was a much-needed morale booster for the family because in Milan three days earlier Dettori's father had broken his leg in two places.

Frankie's distress at the news of his father's accident might have been playing on his mind but it certainly did not show in the way he handled Lizzy Hare. Demonstrating the kind of nerve and judgement that would eventually be honed into the consummate skills of a champion, Dettori brought Lizzy Hare with a dashing run up the inside of the field and popped her in front in the last 100 yards. They beat Interlacing, ridden by Steve Cauthen who was to win his third jockeys' title that year.

'Lanfranco's Hare!', the headline in the *Racing Post* said, and Cumani reveals that his eponymous secretary played a key part in a victory that left Dettori thinking big time. 'I was unable to go to Goodwood, and Frankie was too young to drive, so we had to try to find him a lift,' Cumani says. 'We couldn't find anybody to take him there, so in the end I got Lizzy to drive him down in my car.

'Frankie was obviously pretty elated by his win. When I got back in the car the next day there was a box of Kleenex on the seat and he'd written on it "Frankie goes to Hollywood".'

The neon lights were flashing already.

CHAPTER TWO
BORN UNDER A LUCKY STAR

Frankie Dettori was born in Italy, nurtured in Britain and made in America. The last part of that statement might seem curious, but it refers to the fact that successive visits to the United States during his formative years with Cumani played a major part in honing Dettori's raw talent and imbuing him with the qualities that have made him a champion.

When the British title winner, Steve Cauthen, first arrived in the United Kingdom in 1979 it took him time to adapt to the British tracks and the way the races were run. They said the 'Kentucky Kid' had a clock in his head, a trait possessed by many leading American riders, and Cauthen's remarkable judgement of pace soon overcame his initial difficulties. In 1984 he became the first American champion to win the British jockey's title since Danny Maher in 1908.

One of Cumani's most frequently-quoted sayings is 'Time is only important when you are in prison', referring to the use of times to evaluate races. Nevertheless, when it came to jockeyship Cumani recognised the importance of riding to the clock and, knowing the other benefits that working and competing in the States could bring, he was keen to send Dettori across the Atlantic for some all-American refinement.

Cumani had a valuable connection in the States in Richard Cross, who had been his assistant at Bedford House before setting up as a trainer in California. It was not the first time Cumani had sent youngsters to work with Cross during British winters, but it was the first time Cross had been really impressed.

'Plenty of riders come over and don't gain a lot from being here,' Cross says. 'Frankie had the ability to mimic and he was very soon able to ride in the style of the American riders. When he comes over now you can't tell him from the local jockeys. He was a good rider from the time I first knew him and what impressed me the most about him was his temperament. His general attitude and the way he got on with people made you think he would go places.'

It is an exhilarating sight to watch the work riders, many of them dark-skinned, Spanish-speaking 'Tex–Mex', clad in denim and chaps, hurtling around the picturesque Santa Anita circuit in the warmth of a Californian dawn with the San Gabriel mountains forming a breathtaking backdrop. Dettori's adaptability, allied to his riding skills and his ability to mix, made sure that he was soon an integral part of that colourful scene.

'Luca wanted Frankie to come over here primarily because we measure everything,' Cross explains. 'When he first came he was just exercising horses but then he worked them more and more. Eventually I would say to him "Go threequarters in such and such a time" and he would do it right on the button.

'One of the reasons I believe the American riders are by and large better than the English from an early age is that they have to breeze ten horses in the morning when they are young apprentices, so that by the time they are twenty they have ridden so much more fast work than their English counterparts.'

Like so many other people Dettori became involved with, Cross was taken at least as much with his character as his riding. That might sound bordering on the sycophantic, but it is a genuine appraisal nevertheless.

'The first year Frankie came over he stayed with us in my house in Pasadena, quite close to Santa Anita,' Cross says. 'He was like one of the family. He fitted in so well with my wife and kids. His English was minimal and he was very small, like a schoolboy. I taught him how to play Nintendo and he beat me from then onwards.

'He was an absolute delight to have as a house guest – I think that's the reason for his success. He's one of those people that if you haven't seen for a long time you really look forward to seeing again. He's a charming, charming person and if he ever screwed up in a race he'd charm you so you'd have to put him back on again.'

During his American trips, Dettori also rode a lot for another ex-Brit, Chris Speckert. The Eton-educated Speckert, who is also based at Santa Anita and provided Dettori with his first winner in the States, is equally effusive in discussing the little Italian kid with the winning ways.

'Frankie and his parents rented a house from me in Sierra Madre,' Speckert recalls. 'He rode his first winner in the States on a horse of mine called Smart Dollars and his parents were there in the winner's enclosure with him. They were over the moon and Frankie was obviously pretty excited. I'm part Italian and we had a good, old-fashioned Italian-style party that night in a restaurant in Sierra Madre.

'Frankie was a little wild when he first came over, but I helped settle him down and he became a great friend. Everyone loved him because he was so nice and friendly. He got people on his side. He's got a great heart, he's very kind and he always shows a lot of respect for people.'

Like Cross, Speckert says that Dettori learnt a lot from his stints in the States, mostly by watching and copying the big names. 'He was in awe of the top jockeys like Bill Shoemaker and Angel Cordero and he watched the likes of Cordero and Eddie Delahoussaye closely to see how they rode and what made them tick as well,' Speckert says.

'Young riders learn a bit of aggression over here, how to get down and ride instead of sitting up and waiting. We have the best riders in California and to work with them and compete with them you've got to be good. Frankie looked and learnt a lot and he was never smug. He wasn't just another scrawny apprentice. He always had that something about him, that spark, even when he was sixteen.'

Speckert says that Dettori particularly admired Cordero, the flamboyant South American rider, who retired in April 1992, having ridden 7,258 winners in his career, putting him in third place behind Shoemaker and Laffit Pincay on the all-time list. Cordero, who is now training at Belmont Park in New York, remembers how Dettori dedicated his Breeders' Cup win on Barathea to him with that now famous leap.

'Frankie told me that when he jumped off Barathea he was doing it in memory of me,' Cordero says. 'I met Frankie when he was riding over here a few years earlier and him and me and Jorge Velasquez [another leading rider] became good friends. I've ridden against him in Saudi Arabia, New York and California. We always talk a lot when we meet.

'I admire him a lot. He could be champion anywhere. He's a nice guy, too. Good sense of humour, good character and he hasn't let success go to his head.'

Frankie's stateside takeover didn't always go so smoothly. Not everyone was bowled over by his Latin charm. In an interview with Judith Oliver in *Pacemaker Update*, Dettori recalled a humbling encounter with Wayne Lukas, the record-breaking trainer who became the first man to win five straight American classics when Thunder Gulch followed his 1995 Kentucky Derby success with victory in the Belmont Stakes.

'Last year [1988],' Dettori said, 'Richard Cross had a bad year, so I went up to Wayne Lukas and said "Mr Lukas, I'm Lanfranco Dettori, Luca Cumani's apprentice. Would you mind if I came and rode out for you?" He looked me up and down and said "I'm in very good shape, thank you very much". It was really embarrassing.'

In an interview for the *Independent*, Dettori also told me that his working holidays in the States had been a chastening experience. 'You are in the newspapers all the time in Britain,' he said. 'But when you go to America you realise you are just a nobody. You are lucky to get one ride a week at 99-1. It brings you down to earth.'

As far as improving his riding went, Dettori said: 'It was an extremely good experience. I think it helped me improve my style and my judgement of pace. Now that I'm using my whip in an upright position I think I can use it quicker.'

Cumani echoes most of Dettori's comments, citing his sense of pace and the American style which he adapted to British tracks as the main benefits of the

Frankie who? Wayne Lukas, the record-breaking American trainer, was one of the few people unmoved by Dettori's charm when the young Italian spent successive winters in the United States during his apprenticeship.

visits. What Cumani means by the latter part of his statement is that Dettori has not completely resorted to the style of the US riders because although he crouches low down on his mount he is not quite so far up the horse's neck. And whereas the Americans ride 'acey–deucey', with one leather shorter than the other, Dettori is British in his even-legged style.

When Dettori returned from his American winters he was an exceptionally polished young rider, but not yet the finished article. Some of the finer points that would make him champion would only come with experience. It is interesting at this point to get an expert assessment of Dettori's style and ability as it has evolved today from Robert Sidebottom, senior instructor at the British School of Racing in Newmarket.

'We wouldn't recommend our pupils to copy Frankie, because like Lester Piggott he has a very individual style,' Sidebottom says. 'He has his toe in the stirrup instead of his foot and he crouches very low and maintains the position, which gives him the ability to get behind a horse and push it out without getting unbalanced. That takes a lot of physical strength and skill and is not easy to do.'

With his almost horizontal posture and his whip held high up by his head like a car aerial, Dettori is certainly unmistakeable in a race. 'The one area which we would advise young jockeys to copy is Frankie's use of the whip,' Sidebottom says. 'He gives a horse a chance to respond before he hits it and he never overuses the stick.

'I would describe him as an outstanding jockey. He has all the qualities that make a good horseman – style, balance, and an ability to make them switch off and relax. He has an affinity with horses, they run for him. With more experience he can only get better. In time, who's to say he won't be up there with the best half-dozen of the modern era?'

Despite those qualities, it was not a one-way ticket to the top for Dettori. The Frankie Goes to Hollywood syndrome of that first British success on Lizzy Hare had to be put on hold. There were just seven more wins during 1987 and twenty-two in 1988 – hardly earth-shattering stuff.

'It wasn't easy for him, particularly with his Italian name. People probably thought he was just a protégé of mine,' says Cumani.

There was also still a streak of wilfulness and bumptiousness that occasionally got in the way. Cliff Woof, a former professional footballer who was on the books of Liverpool FC, was Dettori's agent during 1988, and he recalls that although he was ambitious Dettori was not happy about being sent all over the place to ride.

'He had a certain arrogance about him,' Woof says. 'If we got him a ride at Carlisle he would say "I'm not going all the way up there for one ride". But top sportsmen need that kind of arrogance in a way. You come across people from time to time who have extreme confidence in their own ability and Frankie had that; he definitely knew where he was going. The nearest thing in football terms would be Paul Gascoigne, although Frankie's not quite as daft as Gazza!'

Woof says that despite Dettori's desire to reach the top he was understandably more interested in doing the normal things teenage boys do, particularly when it involved the local girls. Sporting a fringe haircut that made him resemble an Italian Beatle, Dettori's Latin looks made him as different from the local lads as lasagne from Lancashire hotpot, and he was certainly not lacking in smooth talk even if it was in broken English.

'He was living in digs in All Saints Road in Newmarket, but he was never there for more than five minutes,' Woof says. 'He was always difficult to track down when we wanted to book him for a ride. He was a chirpy little guy, who was always full of fun. A lot of jockeys, even the young ones, drive BMWs or Mercs, but Frankie used to float around town on a moped.

'He'd turn up in our office dressed very casually in jeans and football shirts [Dettori is a fanatical supporter of Juventus and Arsenal] and within five minutes he'd turn the place upside down, cracking jokes and generally playing the fool. The thing about Frankie, though, is that he is one of those people whose public image is the same as his private persona. The happy-go-lucky, smiling fellow you see on your TV screens is not a front.'

Dettori admits that he was a bit undisciplined during that period. 'Nineteen eighty-eight was the year I did all my silly things,' he told me in the interview mentioned earlier. That applied on the track as well as off it, as two incidents at Catterick in July that year illustrate fairly graphically.

On the first occasion, Dettori was riding an odds-on favourite called Casey and having gone clear he eased up near the line and only just held on in a photo-finish. Dettori came back in aboard Casey patting his heart and wiping his brow with the kind of theatrical aplomb that has become his trademark. The stewards gave him a stiff talking to and Dettori, as ever finding something to say, remarked: 'I was smiling when I came back in and the stewards told me off. But I was smiling with relief. I have learnt my lesson.'

Gerald Leigh, the owner–breeder of Casey, recalls: 'I was sent a photo of the finish showing Frankie turning and smiling to the camera just before the finish and I said to him "I suppose that's for your mother".'

In the second Catterick incident, Dettori was not treated so leniently. Riding a horse named Torkabar, who started an even hotter favourite at 5-2 on, Dettori finished third and was banned for three days for hitting the horse over the head.

Dettori said at the time: 'I sensed he was going to try to duck through the gate to the paddock so I gave him a tap to try to keep him straight. It was not in anger. It seems a severe punishment. Perhaps they remembered the last meeting here. That's life and I have to take it on the chin.'

Dettori's misery was not over by any means. There was a double wammy when he returned to Cumani's yard in Newmarket, beginning with a suspension from Cumani himself who banned him from riding for a further two weeks. The final ignominy came from Ray Cochrane, Cumani's stable jockey.

Cochrane, a down-to-earth, thoroughly likeable Ulsterman, has ridden the roller-coaster of racing fortune more than most. Born one of seven children in County Down, he was hardly bred to be a top jockey as his father was a painter and decorator and his mother a linen-mill worker.

He had to suffer serious weight problems, two bad accidents, an abortive switch from Flat racing and back again, and then years of struggling to shake off the label of being just another second-division rider. His ability finally brought him recognition and the coveted job with Cumani which climaxed with his superbly executed Derby triumph on Kahyasi.

Others in Cochrane's position might have tried to keep the cocky little Italian kid in his place, but Cochrane acted more like a big brother and was a constant source of encouragement and inspiration. Despite Dettori's brashness, Cochrane found himself liking him from the word go.

'When Frankie first came to Luca's he was a typical yappy kid,' Cochrane recalls. 'He was full of it, but he had lots of charisma and he was the sort of fellow you took to straight away. He would ask my advice all the time and I would be happy to give it to him, although he didn't really need a lot of it!'

Like Cumani, however, Cochrane recognised that there were times when Dettori needed serious chastening for his own good. So, when a peeved Frankie returned from Catterick still smarting from his punishment, Cochrane quite literally put the boot in.

'I was really pissed off with him over that incident. The horse belonged to one of our most important owners [the Aga Khan],' Cochrane says. 'I went to look for Frankie at evening stables. It was about six-thirty in the evening and it was pouring with rain. Frankie was scratching around in one of the boxes. He had a fork in his hand and he was supposed to be mucking out, but quite honestly he was always more interested in riding than mucking out.

'I went over to him and kicked him hard up the arse – he went about four feet in the air. I warned him about ever doing anything like it again. It sunk in alright because he got up and started doing some serious mucking out. There was manure flying about everywhere.'

In contrast to that painful lesson, Cochrane was to do Dettori the biggest favour of his life the following year, as we shall see. But, even before Cochrane played Santa Claus, 1989 proved to be the year that Dettori's career really took off. He became champion apprentice with a total of seventy-five winners, equalling the post-war record set by Edward Hide, and began regularly to make

Ray Cochrane, who offered Dettori friendship, guidance and a kick up the backside during his early career with Luca Cumani.

35

the headlines in the racing press.

At one stage that year, however, it looked as if Dettori might be upstaged by another exceptionally talented rider named Alan Munro, who had also adopted the streamlined American style. Munro, who is three years older than Frankie, found his career taking off at a relatively late stage after he won the Lincoln Handicap at Doncaster on Evichstar in 1990.

The following year, riding as first jockey for the Saudi prince Fahd Salman, Munro rode the brilliant colt, Generous, to victories in the Derby, Irish Derby and King George VI and Queen Elizabeth Diamond Stakes. In 1989, though, it was the race for the title of champion apprentice that Munro dominated for a while, setting the pace in the early months of the season with Dettori struggling in his wake.

By the beginning of June, Dettori had nosed in front of Munro with the help of his first treble, at Leicester. It was a momentous afternoon for him because he had his apprentice allowance reduced from 5lb to 3lb through the first of those three winners, a horse named Versailles Road.

The horse was trained by Susan Piggott, who had taken over the licence from Lester while he served his year in jail for tax evasion. Little did anyone suspect that Lester would make his astonishing comeback to race riding at the same course just sixteen months later at the age of 54.

The Piggotts were long-time friends of Gianfranco Dettori and, not to be outdone, Dettori senior had shown himself to be almost as ageless as Piggott when he won the Italian 2,000 Guineas on Sikeston a few weeks earlier at the age of 49. Versailles Road was Frankie's first mount for the Piggotts and Susan said: 'That was his first ride for us, but it won't be his last. He was excellent today.'

Susan, who had suffered life-threatening injuries when thrown from her pony, Pepe, while Lester was in prison – he was allowed out to visit her – can be as uncommunicative as Lester, which is perhaps understandable in view of the constant intrusions into their lives from media men pursuing Piggott stories. However, she is more than willing to open up when it comes to discussing Dettori.

'Frankie is a tremendous jockey. He has an enormous amount of natural ability and the aptitude to make the best of it,' Susan says. 'One sees so many people over the years with great ability but they don't know how to maximise it. They lack the quick thinking that enables them to decide to go for a gap when it appears and they don't have the clock in their head which Frankie has.

'Frankie is a very intelligent boy with a wonderful sunny attitude to everything. He seems to have that *joie de vivre* in everything he does. Everybody gets days when they are a bit down, but Frankie just loves doing what he is doing. He loves riding winners and he seems to get as much pleasure from winning a seller at Wolverhampton as winning a classic.'

Old pals act: Frankie's father Gianfranco (right) was great friends with Lester Piggott and his wife Susan, who compares Frankie favourably with Lester.

At one point Dettori looked like being plagued with the same kind of chronic weight problem that beset Lester. Both men shared a liking for sweet things particularly ice cream, and Frankie was dubbed the 'Chocolate Mousse Kid' by the *Sun* newspaper because of his apparent habit of celebrating victory with a tub of the stuff.

Susan Piggott sees certain similarities between her husband and Dettori. 'Frankie has his weight under control now, but at one point he was shooting up in height and you wondered if weight would be a real problem. Frankie has the same build as Lester and they are both possessed of similar determination. I know that Lester thinks an awful lot of Frankie as a jockey.'

These days Dettori can ride at 8st 4lb at a push, but he is more comfortable at around 8st 6lb. He is only slightly taller than the average jockey and not quite in the 'Long Fellow' category of Piggott.

After the Leicester highpoint there was no holding Dettori, and Munro was the one left floundering as the young Italian booted home doubles and trebles as if they were going out of fashion. After a Sandown treble in June, the *Racing Post* carried the headline 'Dettori is poised to be champion on treble showing', and later that month another threesome, at Nottingham, took his seasonal tally to twenty-eight, double the score of Munro, who was his nearest pursuer.

The phone bill to his father was taking a fair chunk of his earnings. They kept in touch on a regular basis and after the Nottingham successes he said: 'I rang my father in Italy and he couldn't believe it when I told him how many winners I'd been riding.'

Gianfranco was very soon to hear something far more astonishing coming down the wires, but before that, in July, Versailles Road helped Dettori to another landmark when he won at Beverley. Watching him punching the air in triumph as he passed the post, you would have thought he had won a classic instead of a minor event at the Yorkshire track.

Dettori was celebrating the loss of his right to claim the 3lb allowance, racing's version of the transition from boyhood to manhood. Whether any young rider should celebrate that moment of weightlessness is a moot point because the allowance is what makes an apprentice attractive to trainers when they are seeking to remove poundage from their horses' backs.

Very often a promising youngster can slip from temporary stardom into obscurity when losing the right to claim, as Brough Scott highlighted in an article in the *Sunday Times* in July 1989. 'He crouches low, he is going fast, but history shows Frankie Dettori's game could also be snakes and ladders,' wrote Scott.

'The winners are coming on at the flood ... the phone is ringing, the praise is lavish, the smile is easy,' Scott continued. 'At 18, Frankie is the season's teenage shooting star. But can he, against the trend, continue the climb to the very top of the board? The facts are not encouraging. Since a youthful Pat Eddery led the table in 1971, no other champion apprentice has made it into the highest class.'

Scott went on to list a clutch of promising riders, including Robert Edmondson, David Dineley, Alan Bond, Jimmy Bleasdale and Gary Bardwell, who had all won the apprentice title in recent years, but for one reason or another were struggling to survive or had given up altogether. Dettori was fully aware of the dangers, but that did not prevent him tempering caution with a typical statement of self-belief, and indeed self-promotion.

'Now comes the crunch,' he was quoted as saying after Versailles Road did the business for him. Then he added: 'I think I'm riding better than last year and confidence is a great help. I still hope to get as many rides now. I'm very happy with Mr Cumani and would love to stay, but obviously if the offer of a top job came along I would have to consider it.'

To be fair to Dettori, you could not blame him for putting his credentials in the shop window. His prospects of obtaining the number one position with Cumani seemed zero. Cochrane was still riding as well as ever and seemingly content to remain indefinitely at Bedford House where the team of horses was as good as, if not better than, it had ever been, both in terms of quality and quantity.

Out of the blue, just five weeks after Dettori lost his claim, came an announcement that stunned the racing world on two counts. On the morning of 29 August 1989 the front pages of the *Racing Post* and the *Sporting Life* carried the news that Cochrane was to leave Cumani to be stable jockey for Guy Harwood, the highly successful Sussex trainer – and Dettori, at the tender age of 18, was named as his successor.

Appointing such a relatively inexperienced rider to this high-profile position, where he would be riding for some of the most important patrons of the international racing scene, seemed a major gamble on Cumani's part and some might have put it even more strongly than that. But Cumani never had a moment's doubt that the understudy was ready to take over the lead role and play it with total conviction.

Cumani's public statement said: 'I'm sorry to see Ray go. I have spoken to my owners and we have decided Frankie Dettori will be number one for the stable next season. For next year, at least, there will be one proviso, that for pressure rides and some big races he may be asked to step down for someone more experienced. I am sure he will fit into the role with no problems. I have every confidence in his ability to do the job well.'

The proviso Cumani mentioned might have seemed anything but a full vote of confidence. Asking Dettori to step aside on the big occasions surely placed a question-mark against his readiness for the job in a big way. But Cumani says the wording was merely political.

'For my part there was absolutely no agonising over the decision,' Cumani explains. 'I was absolutely certain Frankie was ready. It was just a question of whether I could convince the owners and most of them did not need much convincing. The proviso about the big races was put in only to keep some of them happy.'

There were certainly precedents at the highest level for Dettori's elevation. Lester Piggott was only 18 when he became first jockey to Sir Noel Murless, still regarded by many as the greatest British trainer this century. Walter Swinburn, three times winner of the Derby, was 19 when he became number one for Michael Stoute's championship-winning Newmarket yard, and Pat Eddery was 20 when he moved into the hot seat for Peter Walwyn.

Confident as ever in his own ability, Dettori said at the time: 'The pressure is really on Luca Cumani who has given me the chance. But I think I will always be able to satisfy him and I will always be trying my best. When I told my father about the new job he thought I was maybe a little too young to take it on, but

Pointing to the future: Dettori secured the plum job as stable jockey to Luca Cumani at the age of 18 when Ray Cochrane left to join Guy Harwood.

you can't turn away an opportunity like this, can you? I'm very excited about it. I couldn't sleep when I was told I was going to be number one.'

As Dettori said, his father clearly believed it was far too soon for his son to be entrusted with the reins and he told him of his concerns when they spoke about the offer. However, Dettori senior confined himself to saying publicly: 'If he carries on as he has done and takes things seriously he will be successful. He will encounter problems, but he will come through them the way he has always done.'

There were others, apart from his father, who seriously doubted whether Dettori was ready for the challenge, both emotionally and professionally. The worry was that such a sudden exposure to the fame and fortune the Cumani position offered might turn the young Dettori's head and cause him to squander his talent as others before him have done in similar circumstances.

One of the doubters was Gerald Leigh, who recalls flying up to Newcastle with Dettori shortly after he had found out about his promotion. 'I flew up to Newcastle races with Frankie, Walter Swinburn and John Hills,' says Leigh. 'Frankie couldn't wait to tell me about it. He was very excited and he said "Guvnor, guvnor, have you heard the news? I've been made stable jockey".'

'I said to Frankie, "I think you've been made stable jockey too soon. It will be difficult for you. Be careful – it could be the undoing of you." After that Frankie went very quiet and he was very thoughtful for the rest of the journey.'

Too young or not, things moved ahead at an even faster pace than anyone could have anticipated. Shortly after Dettori's appointment, Cochrane broke his collarbone in a dramatic incident in the Portland Handicap at Doncaster, which ended the careers of Paul Cook and Ian Johnson. Drainage problems caused the track to subside, causing a dreadful tangle of fallen horses and riders that could easily have ended with a fatality. Cook successfully sued the owners of Doncaster racetrack and in 1995 he received a substantial sum in damages. Cochrane settled out of court and Johnson is still pursuing the matter.

Cochrane's accident, which kept him out for a month, meant Dettori took over on several of the plum end-of-season rides for Cumani, beginning with a first classic mount on N C Owen in the St Leger, which was switched to Ayr from Doncaster because of the subsidence. There was no high-grade start to Dettori's classical education as N C Owen trailed home a well-beaten sixth to Michelozzo, but merely playing a part at such a heady level had its reward.

The extra winners that resulted from Cochrane's absence helped Dettori equal Hide's record score of seventy-five, but almost more important in career terms was a clutch of rides at the very highest level that provided him with invaluable experience and exposure. Despite his depth of self-confidence Dettori has never been too proud to ask advice, and when he sought advice from Cochrane about how to approach his new role Cochrane was only too happy to give it.

'I used to tell him to go out there and not worry about it,' Cochrane says. 'I just told him, "Ride your race with confidence and if you win, you win".'

Dettori didn't win any of the glittering prizes on Prix de l'Arc de Triomphe weekend in October, but he enjoyed an exciting forty-eight hours as an also-ran. He took over on Legal Case in the Arc, Europe's premier all-aged middle-distance event, and Statoblest in the Prix de l'Abbaye de Longchamp, the big sprint on Arc day. He also rode Cullinan in Europe's richest two-year-old event, the Cartier Million in Ireland.

As Dettori played the role of onlooker, a flame-haired Irishman by the name of Michael Kinane signalled his arrival as the supreme jockey for the big occasion when he won the Arc on Carroll House and the Cartier Million on The Caretaker, a double that netted him more than some jockeys make in years of hard graft.

While Kinane took the plaudits on the Longchamp victory podium after the Arc, Dettori was quietly showering and changing before flying back from Paris to Newmarket with little more to show for his efforts than his riding fees and a pair of grubby riding breeches. Or so it might have seemed.

Cumani sees the sequence of events that projected Dettori so swiftly into the spotlight as more than just the natural flowering of an outstanding talent. He alludes to other occasions when fate stepped in to give Dettori a leg up, including the ultimate in 'spare rides', as we shall see.

'Don't get me wrong, Frankie has always worked hard at it and he always had the ability,' Cumani says. 'But when he was my second jockey, Ray was twice injured in falls and both times it coincided with my horses being in top form for good races and Frankie was on them. He does have this amazing penchant for being in the right place at the right time. I've always said Frankie was born under a lucky star.'

Fair comment, perhaps, but some would say that the true brilliance of Italy's little shooting star was that he made his own luck.

CHAPTER THREE
PRAYERS, PIGGOTT AND THE POPE

Many sportsmen and women have superstitions, rituals or religious faith to buoy them up on the big occasion and jockeys are no exception. In the high-pressure world of horse racing where by the very nature of the sport riders face the possibility of serious injury daily, the ultimate example of enlisting the power of a higher authority is the top American rider, Pat Day, who is a lay preacher and acts as a kind of unofficial padre for the riders in the States.

During the 1990 Breeders' Cup in New York three horses were killed in horrific accidents in two of the first three races on the card. Riders were going down like tin soldiers in a shooting gallery and it was amazing that there were no serious human casualties. To calm frayed nerves, Day suddenly stood up in the weighing room and asked all the jockeys to gather round. 'There's been a lot of shit going down today. It's time we got someone on our side,' he said.

Day then bowed his head and prayed: 'Dear Lord, protect these fine riders and their trusting mounts'. He recited the Lord's Prayer and said 'Amen'. There were high-fives and a few shouts of 'Hallelujah!' and 'Alright!' and it was back to business.

Such a scene could only happen in the States, perhaps, but in a less public way quite a few British-based riders look for divine help and inspiration, including Frankie Dettori who has his own, very personal approach.

At the beginning of each season Dettori pays a special visit to church to pray to the Madonna di Montenero and ask for safe passage through the new campaign. The pilgrim church of Montenero contains a miraculous picture of the Madonna, supposed to have sailed there by itself in 1345 from the island of Negro Pont.

Dettori carries medallions depicting the Madonna in his jockey's bag throughout the long and exhausting round of early-morning workouts on the gallops, endless meetings day and night and thousands of miles of travelling. At the end of the season he returns to church to give thanks to the Madonna for safe deliverance.

When Dettori began his first season as number one to Cumani in 1990, he must have thought his guiding light had deserted him for good. It was no

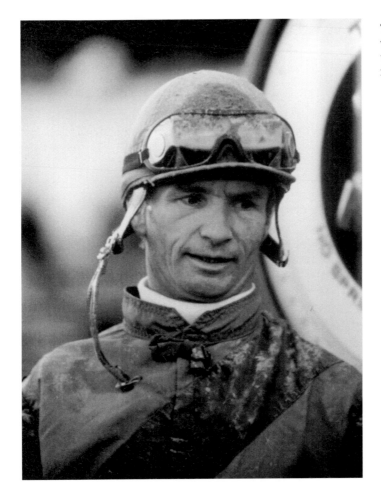

Top American rider Pat Day, who acts as a kind of unofficial padre for his fellow riders.

exaggeration to say that he was exceptionally lucky to escape serious injury and even death in four separate incidents on and off the track.

The trauma began when the season had barely left the starting gate. Riding Long Island in the Princess Elizabeth Stakes at Epsom in April, Dettori became the victim of a reckless move by Michael Hills on Flying Diva, who went for a non-existent gap as the race reached its climax a furlong and a half from the finish.

Flying Diva cannoned into Long Island causing her to somersault three times as she plunged to the ground. Dettori was flung sideways and went crashing through the rail (thankfully made of plastic) in a scene that had onlookers gasping. Long Island broke a shoulder and was put down, while Dettori, having rolled away from the mêlée through the rail, amazingly suffered nothing worse than severe bruising and missed only a couple of days riding.

Hills was suspended for fourteen days and Dettori in a statement that mixed levity with seriousness said: 'Michael apologised to me and there are no hard feelings. It was one of those things – I hope he has learned from it. At least I'm ready for the Grand National now!'

Four weeks later he somehow managed to escape without a scratch when his Mercedes was badly damaged in a crash on the M1 near Nottingham. Another car rammed into the back of Dettori's when it was stationary in a queue of traffic and completely twisted the suspension. He was dozing on the back seat and hardly turned a hair.

Just three days after reshaping his Merc, he was involved in another stomach-churning incident on the track when his mount, Muirfield Village, stumbled and catapulted him out of the saddle during a race at Sandown. He was knocked sideways in mid-air when he collided with another horse and lay motionless on the ground for a long while.

Spectators feared he was seriously hurt, but after being stretchered off the track he was found to have no lasting damage, although he was off for four days. 'When I woke up the next day I felt as if I had been run over by a lorry,' he said. 'Next time I ride I'll wear a body protector.'

That was not the end of the saga, although there was four months' respite before the next bone-crunching incident, at Haydock Park in September. After finishing second on Baylis he was thrown heavily when the horse stumbled after passing the post. This time there was good reason to believe that he had sustained permanent damage because while he lay absolutely still on the turf ambulance staff fitted him with a supportive neck brace before placing him on a stretcher and whisking him to hospital.

In retrospect, the Madonna had obviously been very much alongside him throughout. X-rays showed that once again Dettori had suffered only bruising. After being discharged from hospital he spent the night at Ginger McCain's stables at Southport where he met the triple Grand National winner, Red Rum, for the first time.

McCain's son, Donald, who had been a pupil assistant with Luca Cumani and knew Dettori from his time at Bedford House, picked him up from Warrington Hospital. Knowing Dettori's penchant for the theatrical, you might have expected him to jump up on Red Rum's back and reel off a suitable one-liner, but McCain junior says Dettori was far too sore to do anything very much at all.

Frankie and Rummy were two great survivors together, although unlike the old horse, who was enjoying a well-earned retirement, Dettori still had a major obstacle or two to negotiate as he pursued his relentless climb to the top.

The accidents did not affect his cofidence one iota. He bounced straight back from the Epsom horror show to gain his first Group Two success on a horse named Markofdistinction in the Trusthouse Forte Mile at Sandown three

Dettori has suffered a series of horrific falls during his career in Britain, but has emerged each time with little more than bruising. One of his most dramatic accidents was in the Princess Elizabeth Stakes at Epsom in 1990 (opposite top) when his mount, Long Island, was killed and he crashed through the rail. He also escaped virtually unscathed after falls in 1995 at Kempton Park (opposite bottom) and Haydock Park (right), where he appeared to be seriously hurt as he was stretchered off the track.

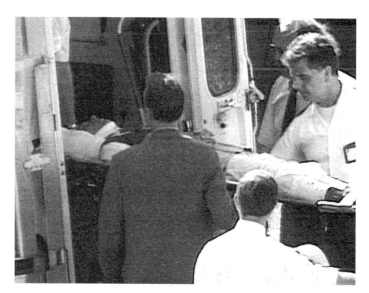

days later. Gerald Leigh, the horse's owner, recalls with amusement that Dettori described the horse as 'the fastest horse what I have ever sat on'.

Markofdistinction had tremendous ability but he had gained a reputation for being something of an awkward character. Dettori fathomed out the way to ride him, kidding him and cajoling him so he hardly knew he had been in a race. Following the Sandown success the partnership brought off two major triumphs, beginning with the Queen Anne Stakes at Royal Ascot, which gave Dettori his breakthrough at the most prestigious meeting of the year.

After wriggling through the field to storm into the lead, he had just enough in hand to hold the late run of Mirror Black, and although there was only a neck in it Dettori was able to raise his whip and smile for the crowd as he passed the post. This time, though, there was no need for Leigh to inject any sarcasm about posing for Mamma.

Racegoers were already getting used to Dettori's theatrical ways and the glamour of Ascot automatically brought out the showman in him. He had tasted the Ascot ambiance first as a skinny 16-year-old when he rode Merle into sixth place for Clive Brittain in the Royal Hunt Cup, or the 'Roylunkah' as he was then calling it.

'It's fantastic, an unbelievable atmosphere with the Queen and everything,' Dettori said at the time. 'I hadn't heard of it before I came to the UK, but it's like the Cup Final. It's got to be the best meeting in the world.'

He was punching the Ascot air even more emphatically three months later after Markofdistinction had given him his first success in a Group One event, one of racing's premier division contests. The race was the Queen Elizabeth II

Getting it off Pat: Dettori gains the first Group One success of his career on
Markofdistinction in Ascot's Queen Elizabeth II Stakes in 1990, beating
Pat Eddery on Distant Relative.

Stakes at Ascot, and Dettori showed all his best qualities to hold off Pat Eddery
on Distant Relative in a gripping finish.

'I've done it – my first Group One success,' he said exultantly. Later that
afternoon he was describing it as 'the greatest day of my life' after Shamshir,
also trained by Cumani, had given him a second Group One win in the Fillies'
Mile.

The presence of his father, who had also been there for the Royal Ascot
triumph, added greatly to Dettori's euphoria. The two hugged fondly after
Markofdistinction's victory before Frankie dashed off to attend the press
conference. Standing up on a chair in the middle of a room crammed full of
hard-bitten pressmen, Dettori – then aged 19 – showed no trace of nerves and
revelled in being centre stage.

'I've got nothing to say,' he announced teasingly, before proceeding to
answer everything that came his way with a maturity and assurance that totally
belied his youth. That he did so came as no surprise to this particular observer.
After I had interviewed him earlier in the year he had the last word when the

interview was over, saying 'Good interview' in a way that made it quite clear who was calling the shots.

A month before his Queen Elizabeth glory day there had been devastation and elation in almost equal measure for Dettori. The death of his friend, 24-year-old Marco Paganini, three-times champion jockey of Italy, after a fall at Grosseto, must have taken the gloss off a remarkable achievement at lowly Chepstow where he surpassed the man many regard as the greatest jockey of all time, Lester Piggott.

In winning the Ferry Stakes on Line of Thunder for Cumani, Dettori became the first teenager to reach a century of winners in a season since Piggott thirty-five years previously. But the icing for Dettori was the fact that he had reached his hundred two months ahead of Piggott, who completed his 'ton' in October, ten days before his twentieth birthday.

After the now obligatory punching of the Welsh air, Dettori said: 'This was just like Royal Ascot. Piggott is the greatest jockey and to beat him by two months is a great achievement. I have been very lucky and everything has gone well. I was not nervous about the challenge of the job because I had seen my father ride so many times.'

Dettori's comment about Piggott being the greatest appeared to be genuine enough; but after Piggott made his remarkable comeback to race riding later that year, lifting the Breeders' Cup Mile on Royal Academy ten days after his return, the young Italian's mocking behaviour might have indicated otherwise.

Dettori's extrovert personality captivated a whole generation of racegoers who had grown used to the sport often being conducted in a sombre, humourless way. The stiff-upper-lip-at-all-times attitude came about largely because racing had been run for so long by an old guard of titled and ex-military gentlemen who regarded it more as a private club than an entertainment business and expected the professionals engaged in it to behave in a gentlemanly fashion.

Dettori arrived not so much as a breath of fresh air as a hurricane and he had already established himself as the prince of pzazz during that first year as number one to Cumani. However, there were those who found his permanently sunny disposition somewhat hard to take and even regarded it as indicative of a lack of application to the job in hand. It was something Dettori alluded to in an interview with Richard Edmondson for the *Independent* in March 1991.

'I do get a lot of stick about being too happy,' Dettori said. 'People say I should settle down; they think I'm not doing the job properly because I'm smiling. But what can I do? I'm full of hope, I love my life and I love my job. Why should I be miserable?

'Lester Piggott has been the biggest thing in British racing for the last fifty years,' he went on. 'People would talk about this brilliant guy who was serious, dedicated, not eating a peanut all day, never smiling or going out. That was the

Pointing the finger: Dettori in playful mood with colleagues Jason Weaver (left) and Richard Fox (centre). Dettori's endless wisecracking and fooling around grated on the nerves of some of the older jockeys.

image in England for so long, so everyone expects you to be like that.'

He certainly did his best to liven 'Old Stoneface' up, as illustrated by Richard Fox, a former jockey renowned for his impishly-Irish sense of humour. Virtually all the younger jockeys, and most of the older ones too, were in awe of Piggott when he returned, but Fox – who was forced to quit riding after breaking a thigh in 1992 – says that not only did Dettori show precious little respect for Piggott, he also drove some of the senior riders to distraction with his antics.

'Everyone else treated Lester with such reverence and there was this young buck taking the mickey,' Fox says. 'Frankie would say things like "Hey Lester, they're going to stuff you and put you in a museum", or once he ruffled his hair and said "Hey Lester, I see you're riding in Milan tomorrow. They love you in Milan. When you die they're going to build a statue of you".

'Another time he stuffed an ice-cream cone in Lester's face and said "Hey Lester, have some ice-cream". Lester just used to ignore him and whisper "He's ****ing mad, isn't he?".'

'Some jockeys, particularly the older ones, used to get a bit fed up with his non-stop talking and his singing,' Fox explains. 'If it wasn't that, he'd be hugging you, kissing you or generally messing you about. It was like looking after your sister's little kid. He's hyperactive, he never stops. He can't just sit down in a corner and mull things over.'

Having said all that, Fox is keen to emphasise that he has high regard for Dettori as a person. 'Frankie helped me a lot. He has a very kind heart. He would always give me a lift to the races to save me money when things weren't going too well for me. Sometimes, if he was flying to a meeting, he'd say "Don't tell anyone. You come on the plane with me".'

Willie Carson, the five-times champion, has been known to show his irritation at Dettori occasionally, but he says quite genuinely: 'Frankie is everyone's friend, he's very popular. When he first arrived on the scene everybody mothered him because he was such a friendly boy and a bit naive. He's not naive now and he's not quite as cheerful as he was because there's more pressure on him.'

Piggott, incidentally, was to get his own back a couple of years later when he parried Dettori's teasing with his own rapier wit. The story goes that when Piggott's personal assistant, Anna Ludlow, was due to have his baby in 1993, Dettori followed Piggott out of the weighing room one day, asking him cheekily 'Hey Lester, what are you going to call this bambino then?'. Piggott walked on straight-faced as Dettori repeated again and again, 'Come on Lester, tell us the baby's name.' Finally Piggott turned round and said, 'Listen Frankie, I don't know what name it'll be, but I'll tell you what – you can be the Godfather!'

As for those irritable folk in the weighing room, no one who makes it to the top in any sphere of life does so without putting a few noses out of joint, mostly through jealousy. There was no doubt that some of the annoyance with Dettori was exacerbated by the green-eyed monster, as he himself recognised when I talked to him around that time. 'Nobody says anything, but you can sense the jealousy,' he said. 'It annoys me because we all started off at the same point, at zero.'

With or without the approval of his weighing room colleagues, Dettori was doing very nicely, *grazie*. He fully justified Cumani's faith in him and finished that first season as the Bedford House number one with a total of 141 winners from 699 rides which put him in fourth place in the table behind Pat Eddery, Willie Carson and Steve Cauthen.

With more and more trainers keen to employ him, there was another first for Dettori when he won on Jahafil for Major Dick Hern. The major, who ranks as one of Britain's greatest post-war classic trainers, is not a man given to displays of elation and will rarely use two words when he can get away with one, but there was no hiding his delight at Dettori's handling of his horse.

'Frankie rode Jahafil exceptionally well. Not that he was a difficult horse to ride, but Frankie did exactly what he was told,' Hern recalls. 'He hasn't had that many rides for me, but he's been very lucky for me. He has virtually a 100 per cent record on my horses. Frankie is a top-class jockey – what more can one say?'

Dettori also filled an annoying gap in his record book when he took the Old Newton Cup at Haydock Park on Hateel, his first win for Peter Walwyn who, it will be recalled, had given him his first mount in Britain. 'I have had a bit of bad luck for Peter Walwyn, so it is good to have my first winner for him,' Dettori said. There was no suggestion to Walwyn on this occasion that his horse was 'fet'.

Dettori was certainly not monopolising the headlines, though. During 1990 there were others who were still capable of nudging the new kid on the block off the front page. Eddery became the first man to ride 200 winners in a season since Sir Gordon Richards in 1952, the year the Irishman was born. Eddery secured his eighth title with a total of 209, while Willie Carson had earlier ridden his 3,000th winner in Britain and notched up his eighteenth century in nineteen seasons.

And on the day Piggott returned to racing under the headline 'Leicester Piggott!', it was announced that Steve Cauthen had signed a retainer with the leading owner, Sheikh Mohammed al Maktoum. Cauthen was following in the footsteps of Eddery and Carson, who had set the trend for jockeys having contracts with owners rather than trainers by signing up with Prince Khalid Abdullah and Sheikh Mohammed's brother, Sheikh Hamdan al Maktoum, respectively. The decision of Sheikh Mohammed to employ a retained jockey was to have significant repercussions for Dettori, as we shall see.

Having made such a success of his first season in the Bedford House hotseat, it might have been expected that Dettori would rise to even greater heights in 1991, but nothing is ever certain in racing's roller-coaster and there was a major setback for the yard that neither Dettori nor Cumani could possibly have anticipated.

In December 1990, the Aga Khan announced that he was to withdraw all the horses he had in training in England as a protest against the disqualification of his filly, Aliysa, from the Oaks the previous year. Minute substances of a banned substance, a derivative of camphor, were found in a post-race test on Aliysa and the Aga stated that he would not have another runner in England until he and his scientists were satisfied that the scientific management of British racing matched the high standards found in other sports. (The Aga signalled an end to his self-imposed exile when he ran a horse calld Adjareli at Royal Ascot in 1995.)

The Aga Khan leads in his 1989 Oaks winner Aliysa. He withdrew his horses in training in Britain after Aliysa was disqualified for failing a dope test.

The principal sufferers from the Aga's action were Cumani, who had trained Kahyasi to win the Derby, and Michael Stoute, who had won two Derbys for him with Shergar and Shahrastani. The Aga had ninety horses split between the two men in Newmarket, and the loss of those horses at a time when the recession was beginning to bite and new owners were proving as difficult to come by as cheques from bookmakers, was a serious blow.

In the mid-eighties Cumani's equine strength had reached a heady peak with around 200 horses in his yard. The dual effect of the Aga's withdrawal and the lack of new owners with money to squander on pricey racehorses saw his numbers decline at an alarming rate, at one point dipping to half that figure.

Naturally this had a marked effect on the quality and quantity of mounts

Cumani could provide for Dettori. And when a jockey's principal retainer is not as productive as it should be, it frequently has a knock-on effect, with outside rides proving proportionately hard to come by as the rate of exposure slows down.

So, after the sustained success of 1990, Dettori found the following season something of an anticlimax. Winners were coming in a trickle at the start and he had ridden only twenty-eight by the end of June and was languishing in eighteenth place in the jockeys' table. He picked up a little in the second half of the year and finished seventh in the list behind Eddery with a total of 94 successes from 707 rides.

It certainly wasn't a totally downbeat campaign, by any means. In a year that

Dettori drives Second Set to victory in the 1991 Sussex Stakes at Goodwood, one of the highlights of a relatively disappointing year for him.

saw Alan Munro win the Derby on Generous and Pat Eddery become only the fifth man to ride 3,000 winners in Britain, there were a few acceptable little tit-bits for Dettori as well.

He made his first impact on the classic scene when he finished third in the 1,000 Guineas on Crystal Gazing and second in the Oaks on Shamshir, both trained by Cumani. And in July he rode his first Derby winner when he took the German version on Temporal.

Later that month, at Glorious Goodwood, when many of Cumani's horses had been laid low by a virus, the two Italians teamed up for a magnificent success in the meeting's main event, the Sussex Stakes, with Second Set and followed up with Tidemark in the Tote Gold Trophy. Sadly, Second Set failed to reproduce that brilliance when Dettori rode him in the Breeders' Cup Mile in Kentucky in November.

There were two rides that gave Dettori particular pleasure. The first was his win on Nibbs Point in the Galtres Stakes at York in which he gave Cumani's filly a brilliant ride to edge out his old rival, Munro, on Always Friendly. Nibbs Point was wandering about as she came under pressure, so Dettori put his whip down and pushed her out with hands and heels to collar Munro in the last twenty yards.

Cumani recalls: 'Frankie showed tremendous grit and determination. Nibbs Point was a very lazy filly and three furlongs out I thought there was no way she could win. But Frankie somehow got her there. He rode a superb race.'

The second was his victory on Mata Cara in the Frankie Dettori Ton-Up Stakes at Chepstow, instituted as a result of his quickfire century the previous season. Not many riders can claim to have a race named after them and, wearing the colours of Sheikh Mohammed, Dettori loved every second of his Welsh rarebit.

There was a much more cosmopolitan triumph awaiting Dettori at the start of 1992. In company with Munro he took on ten riders from Ireland, America, Canada and Japan in the inaugural Young Jockeys' World Championship at Nakayama in Japan in March. With one winner and two seconds Dettori easily lifted the title ahead of the local hero, Norihiro Yokohama.

He was well and truly upstaged by Munro a few days later when Munro was voted Jockey of the Year by his fellow riders. Munro received his award at the annual event that has become known as the Lesters after the inimitable Piggott, who had been given a tumultuous reception when he stepped forward to receive a special Sports Person of the Year award at the inaugural ceremony twelve months previously.

Dettori had quite a bit to chew over apart from his meal as he observed the proceedings. In a separate poll of *Racing Post* readers for the top jockey of the year, he failed to make the top fifteen behind Richard Quinn. Clearly he had a way to go before winning over the British public entirely.

Power play: Dettori shows an outstanding combination of style and strength to win York's
Galtres Stakes on Nibbs Point in 1991.

Dettori's innate self-belief was still as great as ever, but occasionally it would manifest itself in ways that might best be described as over-assertive. That trait was to cost him a first British classic success in May when he forfeited not only the winning ride on Rodrigo de Triano in the 2,000 Guineas but a gilt-edged contract as well through a piece of misguided wheeler-dealing with the man who was a past master at it.

Robert Sangster, the dominant British owner for the best part of a decade until the petro-dollar purchasing power of Sheikh Mohammed and his brothers made him almost a bystander, wanted to take second claim on Dettori's services, but found the 21-year-old trying to outmanoeuvre him at the negotiating table.

Bearing in mind Sangster's business acumen – he was the first man to turn horse racing into a highly lucrative commercial enterprise – that was a very foolish thing to do on Dettori's part.

Sangster, who had brought Steve Cauthen over from the United States to ride for him in 1979, says: 'I was looking for a young jockey and I thought Frankie was the best around. I had a meeting with Frankie and Luca, the idea being that Luca would still have first claim on him and I would have second claim. Frankie insisted on riding Rodrigo de Triano in the Guineas, but I said "No, he's Willie Carson's ride".

'But Frankie still insisted that he had to ride Rodrigo and so we failed to reach an agreement. I had told Frankie that it was very likely that Willie would probably be claimed to ride for the Maktoums in the Guineas anyway, but he chose to ignore it. Luca said he was crazy to do what he did.'

Sangster's attempt to tip Dettori the wink about Carson proved absolutely spot-on because he was claimed to ride Muhtarram for Sheikh Hamdan al Maktoum in the 2,000 Guineas. Dettori ended up riding Badie for John Dunlop

Golden oldie: Lester Piggott wins his thirtieth British classic, the 1992 2,000 Guineas, on Rodrigo de Triano. Dettori, who could have ridden the winner, finishes towards the back on Badie.

and watched from the back of the field as Piggott, the late replacement for Carson, turned back the years in fairy-tale fashion to glide home on Rodrigo.

It was Piggott's thirtieth classic win and Dettori's remarks about putting the 'old man' in a museum must have come back to haunt him as Newmarket gave the 56-year-old grandfather one of the most emotional receptions ever seen on a British racecourse.

Many young jockeys would have been tempted to jump off the stands after forfeiting a lucrative deal with a powerful patron like Sangster. But Dettori, as ever, shrugged off the episode as if it was of no consequence and moved on with hardly a glance backwards, convinced in his own inimitably self-possessed way that it would all turn out for the best.

In the event it was a good season, but not an outstanding one for Dettori, who reached his century with a week of the turf season left and ended with a final tally of 101. The thought that he might have been the man aboard Rodrigo de Triano instead of Piggott when Sangster's brilliant colt added victories in the Irish 2,000 Guineas, the International Stakes and the Champion Stakes, must have niggled just a little bit, but Dettori's eager young eyes had new horizons to focus on.

A first mount in the Derby on the Sandown Classic Trial winner, Pollen Count, had the adrenaline surging as he pulled on Sheikh Mohammed's crimson and white silks and thought of just what it would mean to lift the world's most famous Flat race.

Bearing in mind that his father had been criticised for his riding of Wollow in the 1976 Derby, a victory to redress the family honour would be that little bit sweeter. And as Dettori made his way across the downs to that famous mile and a half start through the gypsies and the day-trippers, with his father watching from the stands, he must have had real hope in an open year that Pollen Count might be good enough.

Having raced prominently until the field swept round Tattenham Corner into the straight, Pollen Count dropped away and trailed home sixteenth of eighteen behind Rodrigo de Triano's stable companion, Dr Devious. The disappointment was soon forgotten, however, when Dettori roared home to win the French Derby four days later on the 37–1 outsider, Polytain.

The Chantilly unsaddling enclosure resembled a little corner of Italy as Dettori indulged in a wild bout of congratulations with Polytain's connections. The horse was trained by the Italian-born Antonio Spanu and owned by the wife of a Paris-based Italian, Bruno Houillion.

The owner, trainer and Dettori's father all came from the same part of Sardinia, and as the Polytain party began some serious celebrating they were unaware that Dettori senior, then 51, was doing his bit for the Sardinian connection by winning the Premio Emilio Turati in Milan on Misil the same afternoon.

Gianfranco retired three months later after more than thirty years in the

Italian job: Dettori wins the 1992 French Derby on the 37–1 outsider Polytain, trained by fellow Italian Antonio Spanu.

saddle and thirteen Italian championships. It will be remembered that he began his career with Cumani's father, Sergio, and Cumani sent four horses to Milan for Dettori senior to ride on his last day in the saddle. He won on two of them before bidding farewell to his adoring public in an emotional scene. Although he made a fleeting comeback two weeks later, he finally left the international stage to young Frankie for good.

Dettori junior, meanwhile, had been lapping up the plaudits of the topper-and-tails brigade by winning his first Ascot Gold Cup on the much-travelled Drum Taps. Riding the hot favourite, Arzanni, Dettori had been narrowly beaten into second place by Walter Swinburn on the 25–1 chance, Indian Queen, in the previous year's Gold Cup. Handling Drum Taps with a blend of patience and strength, Dettori took his revenge with a perfectly judged success over Swinburn's mount, Arcadian Heights.

As the pair made their move rounding the home turn, Swinburn saved

Move over, maestro: Dettori on Red Slippers (far side) inches out Lester Piggott
on Feminine Wiles in the 1992 Sun Chariot Stakes at Newmarket.

Dettori a painful legacy. Arcadian Heights, who was to win the Gold Cup two
years later, is an aggressive individual who might best be described as an equine
version of Jaws. As Drum Taps raced by him on the bend he swung his head
sideways and tried to take a bite out of Dettori's bottom. Swinburn screamed a
warning and a puzzled Dettori initially thought it was some bizarre form of
gamesmanship on his rival's part.

A ride that must have given Dettori as much pleasure as anything that season
was his victory on Red Slippers in Newmarket's Sun Chariot Stakes in which
he held off Piggott on Feminine Wiles in a pulsating climax. It was not reported
whether the two men had exchanged pleasantries afterwards, but even Piggott
must have been impressed by Dettori's strength and determination. The *Racing
Post* reporter certainly was, saying of the performance: 'Frankie Dettori now
looks the finished article.'

Maybe he was, but in championship terms he was still just part of the supporting cast. The season's laurels were all heading in the direction of the diminutive South African rider, Michael 'Mouse' Roberts, who was one of the most popular champions for years.

Things hadn't gone nearly so smoothly for Roberts first time around. Having been champion of his country eleven times, Roberts found it difficult to establish himself in Britain when he arrived in 1978 and after one season and a mauling from the press he hurried back home.

Determined to prove himself, Roberts returned in 1986 and this time his talent and his personality gradually enabled him to sway owners, trainers and the public on to his side. He was particularly popular with the racing public who warmed to his sunny smile and his habit of waving beatifically to the crowd which earned him the nickname of 'The Pope'. And when the Pope gave everything in a typical all-action finish, punters felt it was the bookies who didn't have a prayer.

Roberts had been a 100–1 shot to win the title at the start of the 1992 season. Owing to a relentless schedule, the backing of an ever-broader base of trainers and some shrewd bookings by his agent Graham Rock (who had helped himself to the 100–1), Roberts began to leave the title holder, Pat Eddery, struggling in his wake.

Roberts was odds-on for the title by the end of June and as the winners snowballed he became only the fifth man to ride 200 winners in a British season, finishing with a total of 206. He was the first South African to win the title and was one of only six foreign riders (not including Irish jockeys) to lift the British championship. The others were the Americans Lester Reiff, Danny Maher and Steve Cauthen, and the Australians Frank Wootton and Scobie Breasley.

As he watched a beaming Roberts jump down niftily from winner after winner, a certain young Italian was beginning to wonder if he would ever break through the golden-oldie barrier and lift the title even though the ambition to do so burned as fiercely as ever. He would have to wait only two years to receive a positive answer, but not before he got himself into all kinds of problems along the way.

CHAPTER FOUR
THE CHINA SYNDROME

For a young man seeking access to a life of glamour and riches, the world of horse racing offers the possibility of instant gratification. Racing has always been a magnet for the wealthy, the powerful and the famous, so for those from underprivileged backgrounds with little prospect of advancement elsewhere – especially those who are, to use the vogue expression, vertically challenged – the opportunity to become even a peripheral part of the Turf's heady ambiance is a lure that is difficult to resist.

To start as a muck-swilling stable lad, as most do, might seem light years away from the high life they crave, but the promise of public acclaim and a full wallet is always there. Many young apprentice jockeys enjoy lifestyles far in advance of anything they could hope to achieve so rapidly in the world of commerce and industry.

And then there is the social side, with invitations from well-heeled owners, exposure on television and in the newspapers and the opportunity for international travel all contributing to a life in the fast lane. Moreover, because jockeys have always enjoyed a kind of pop-star status within their glitzy world, women hang around them like groupies around rock bands and it is not difficult for any red-blooded lad to attract girlfriends galore.

In a story in a tabloid newspaper a few years ago concerning the sexual exploits of certain jockeys in Newmarket, the headquarters of British Flat racing, one rider was said to have come out with the memorable line: 'You don't have to be good looking in Newmarket. All you have to do is walk down the street with a bag with a whip in it.' Exaggeration or not, he made his point.

Money is what makes it all happen, of course, and pursuit of the ultimate monetary high has led many European riders to take up temporary contracts in Hong Kong, where the dollars flow so freely that even Arab oil sheikhs might seem just averagely wealthy. To state that the Chinese have always enjoyed a flutter would be like saying that the Pope says the odd prayer. The turnover at Hong Kong's two principal racetracks, Happy Valley and Sha Tin, and their many off-course betting centres is so mind boggling that it is almost beyond the comprehension of British racegoers.

In the early days of Hong Kong's betting boom, which began to spiral in the last two decades as it developed the most sophisticated racing set-up in the world, it was said that a typical Hong Kong punter would travel to Happy Valley on a 2p tram ride and then stake a little matter of £20,000 on the day's racing. The Chinese believe it is fate, not luck, that governs whether they win or lose, which perhaps explains their propensity for risking vast sums without batting an eyelid.

To quote some recent statistics, an amazing £21 million was staked on the

All that glitters: Happy Valley racecourse in Hong Kong where punters bet sums of money that are mind-boggling by British standards.

Happier times: Luca Cumani with Dettori in 1991, two years before they parted
company in acrimonious circumstances.

last event of the season at Sha Tin in June 1994. And 90,000 people bet a total
of £128 million on nine races at Sha Tin, which represents two and a half times
the statutory Levy on British racing in one year. For the same season, a record
turnover of £5.66 billion for sixty-nine meetings was recorded.

It follows that the rewards for jockeys in Hong Kong are commensurately
vast. At the beginning of 1993, Michael Kinane was riding there on a
temporary basis and Steve Cauthen was also considering an offer, so an
invitation to participate in this big-money free-for-all would obviously have
been a serious temptation for an emerging young rider. It was against this
background of flashing dollar signs and the attendant glamour that Frankie

Main attraction: Dettori steps up to receive the overall Jockey of the Year award at the annual 'Lesters' dinner in London in March 1995. He also took the Flat Jockey of the Year award for the second year running.

Racing Post

Gerry Cranham

She's my number one: Just two of a series of ecstatic moments for Dettori during his memorable association with the champion sprinter Lochsong. Above, in his inimitable way he celebrates winning York's Nunthorpe Stakes in 1993 and, left, he seals victory with a kiss after the 1994 Palace House Stakes at Newmarket.

Trevor Jones

ABOVE Ascot topper: Dettori tastes the heady feeling of his first success at Royal Ascot as he brings Markofdistinction home to win the Queen Anne Stakes in 1990. He rode the horse to victory in the Queen Elizabeth II Stakes over the same course later in the year to gain his first Group One win.

RIGHT Coming into the cold: An early picture of Dettori in England. His smile belies the fact that he found it extremely difficult to adapt to the climate and the English way of life.

Gerry Cranham

BELOW Dettori powers to his first British classic success on Balanchine in the 1994 Oaks at Epsom. The victory was especially sweet for him as he had been beaten inches in the season's first two classics, the 1,000 and 2,000 Guineas, a few weeks earlier.

RIGHT Like father, like son: Frankie Dettori fights out a nose-to-nose finish with his father, Gianfranco, in Milan in 1991. Gianfranco retired the following year after more than thirty years in the saddle and thirteen Italian championships.

Cavalli e Corse

Mel Fordham

That's how it's done, Steve: Dettori gains his first British success aboard Lizzy Hare at Goodwood in June 1987, showing coolness and judgement to overhaul the three-times champion Steve Cauthen in the last 100 yards.

David Hastings

OPPOSITE Champions together: Dettori drives the Derby winner Lammtarra past Pentire to win the King George VI and Queen Elizabeth Diamond Stakes at Ascot in July 1995. And (bottom) he shows his delight at a success he rates among the best moments of his life.

ABOVE Over the moon, ma'am: Dettori has never been inhibited in his meetings with the Queen and here he holds her hand with both of his in a typically spontaneous gesture as he receives his prize for winning Ascot's King George Stakes on Lammtarra.

RIGHT Dettori has always been popular with the ladies and he is pictured here with girlfriend Catherine Allen at Royal Ascot in 1994.

Trevor Jones

Gerry Cranham

Hey, Lester, how ya doin'? Although Dettori has enormous respect
for Piggott as a jockey it has never stopped him teasing the great
man and sending him up.

Dettori made what appeared to many, and to one man in particular, to be the most thoughtless, misguided decision of his young life.

On 3 February 1993, it was announced that Dettori, then aged 22, had agreed terms to ride for a local trainer, Gary Ng Ping Keung. The deal was thought to be worth £250,000 over two years, not an outstanding amount by Hong Kong standards perhaps, but Dettori doubtless realised there would be perks of all kinds on top of that basic figure.

A week later Dettori spoke publicly about his decision to end his eight-year association with Luca Cumani. 'My whole life as a jockey has been built up while I was with Mr Cumani,' Dettori said. 'And everything I have achieved is thanks to him and his owners who were prepared to give me the chance. They took a big risk when they took me on because I was very young and had a lot to prove.

'I'm sad to be leaving such a good team, but I feel my decision to ride in Hong Kong is the right one. When you see jockeys like Mick Kinane going and Steve Cauthen thinking of going you realise how big racing is over there.'

Dettori concluded by saying that when he returned he would still be only 24 and would have plenty of time to get going in Britain again. He admitted, however, that it would be difficult without the backing of a stable like Cumani's, which still housed a very respectable 120 horses at that time.

Cumani viewed the Hong Kong development with utter incredulity. He had been deeply shaken by the Aga Khan's unexpected body blow, but Dettori's move was a far more personal slight and cut like a knife. What made it all the more hurtful was the fact that he learned about it second-hand.

'During that winter Frankie's character had changed,' Cumani explains. 'During previous winters he was always in touch with me, but this time he just disappeared and didn't get in touch at all. Then in January I started reading reports in the papers that he was about to sign up for the Hong Kong deal.

'I was very angry that he hadn't been in touch and hadn't even talked it over with me, but it was far more than that. There was a great sadness for me. There was somebody on the brink of being the best in Europe and he was throwing it away for the glitter of Hong Kong. That was my real frustration – I thought he had champion potential as a jockey and a person.'

Dettori finally reappeared in March and went to see Cumani at Bedford House. It was like a meeting between an angry father and an errant son, with the father seeking to discipline and reproach in a paternalistic rather than a punitive way and the son sticking to his guns, determined to show that he was man enough to make his own decisions without help or guidance from anyone.

'When Frankie came to see me in March I was pretty furious,' Cumani recalls. 'He came in and just laid it down to me. He said "It's no use trying to change my mind. I've done it, I'm going". I said to him "I think it's a waste of your career. You should change your mind".

'I got thoroughly cross with him. I thought the only thing I could do was to shock him a bit. So I said "I just don't want to talk to you. If I can't change your mind I don't want to have anything more to do with you". I literally didn't talk to him from that moment on. I ignored him for almost a year.'

So Dettori had lost a mentor, a friend and, with no disrespect to Gianfranco, a kind of surrogate father as well. If he cared it certainly didn't show, apart from that rather glib public expression of sadness. From his point of view there was no need to look back, only forward. He was young, good looking and gifted, and the world – at least racing's brave new glitzy world – was his oyster. That was how it seemed, but he never got to reach inside for the pearl.

At the time Dettori's Hong Kong agreement had been revealed, the HK Jockey Club had expressed reservations about giving him a licence to ride there. The HKJC were busy compiling a huge dossier on Dettori, and Philip Johnston, the Director of Racing, said somewhat cryptically: 'We see Hong Kong as an important part of an individual jockey's career. We don't see it as a one-off situation.'

It was made clear that Dettori faced a fairly lengthy wait to see if his contract would be approved and he was advised not to sever his ties with Great Britain. But the bridges had been burned and, for the moment at least, Dettori was out on his own in the treacherous waters of racing's vast and frequently intractable sea.

He had begun the year well by winning the World Young Jockeys' Championship in Japan for the second year running, which helped to maintain his high profile as the season started. He also had pledges of support from successful trainers like Lord Huntingdon, Julie Cecil and Clive Brittain; but riding as a freelance has always been a difficult business and with most of the major trainers and owners having made arrangements with other leading jockeys, Dettori seemingly faced a crossroads in his career.

Furthermore, the door at Bedford House had been slammed firmly shut with the news that Ray Cochrane had returned as first jockey for Cumani. The trainer welcomed him back by saying: 'The only reason Ray left was because Frankie was up and coming and he was offered a good job with Guy Harwood. We parted on good terms and it's great to have him back.'

The lucky star that Cumani had spoken of was suddenly obscured by cloud. Having been quoted in the 50–1 bar category for the jockeys' championship, Dettori received a seven-day ban for careless riding at Leicester at the end of April and five days later he incurred a four-day suspension for misuse of his whip on Dayflower when he rode her into fifth place behind Sayyedati in the 1,000 Guineas.

He was serving these two sentences consecutively in May when he was hit by a revelation that appeared to deal him a savage blow, but which, ironically, worked in his favour.

Stories appeared in the press linking Dettori with an alleged drugs incident that threatened to derail his lucrative Hong Kong deal. He was remanded on bail after being arrested on suspicion of possessing drugs in London the previous month. A police spokeswoman said: 'A 22-year-old man went back to Marylebone this morning and was given a police caution for being in possession of a controlled drug. The substance involved was a small amount of cocaine.'

Dettori was given a caution but was not charged when he subsequently reappeared at Marylebone Police Station and he denied any involvement with drugs. 'It wasn't me. The whole thing has been a mix-up,' he said. 'Nobody could prove anything as I have done nothing wrong. I don't take drugs, I am not that stupid. I will admit to having a sleepless night as I knew there was a problem with the police, but it did not concern me. I have done nothing wrong. I am in the clear.'

Despite Dettori's protestations, the incident was enough to concentrate the minds of the HKJC. Two weeks later, following a 90-minute meeting which approved Hong Kong permits for the British riders Gary Carter and Dean McKeown, it was announced that Dettori had been refused a licence. Johnston said: 'We are prepared to entertain a future application, but the licensing committee decided it was not in Dettori's interests or the interests of Hong Kong racing to have him riding here next season.'

Having received the chop from Hong Kong, Dettori's career prospects seemed to be at an all time low. It was not so much a case of being up the creek without a paddle as marooned without a boat. Yet again, though, he shrugged off this latest bombshell as if it were merely the most minor inconvenience.

Perhaps it was a case of whistling in the dark, but on the day of the announcement from Hong Kong, he was seen laughing and joking at Folkestone races as if he had just received a major boost to his career rather than a rejection. Clearly he was prescient as well as self-confident.

Following the announcement of the HKJC's decision, Cumani had made a fairly damning public statement. 'Probably in the long term it's the best thing that could have happened to Frankie,' he said. 'It will teach him how to knuckle down, to grow up and get on with some hard work. He should realise his responsibilities now, concentrate on hard work and forget about making easy money.'

Looking back, Cumani gives a fascinating insight into the psychological processes that led Dettori to make his apparently rash move. 'It was a difficult time for Frankie,' Cumani says. 'The previous year as my jockey he thought he was the bee's knees and he believed everything was due to him. So, for example, he didn't feel he should have to go all the way to Carlisle for just one ride. Then, having been almost part of my family he was suddenly out on his own.

'It was a transitional period from being a kid to becoming a man. That happens to everybody in life. You're neither a man nor a boy and you lose your way slightly. The Hong Kong incident was the best thing that could have happened because it forced him to make the transition.'

Cumani goes on to explain that beneath Dettori's permanently sunny exterior there was a great deal of turmoil. 'Frankie has a very exuberant character, but like most people who have that trait and appear to be on a high all the time, there were also occasions when he had some tremendous lows as well. When he finished his apprenticeship he was on a roller-coaster of highs and lows.'

If that was the case, Dettori certainly showed he had the mental toughness to ride out what could have been the biggest trough of the lot. From being down on the canvas he pulled himself up by his bootstraps and made an extraordinary success of a season that had looked like becoming a washout.

In June he secured his second Derby ride on Wolf Prince, a rare challenger from the United States. Wolf Prince was trained by Michael Dickinson, the former champion jumps trainer in Britain who had been set up as private trainer to Robert Sangster at his magnificent Manton complex, but sacked after just one season. Dettori failed to make any impression on the American invader, but he was not too dejected as his Derby day had earlier been highlighted by a glittering success for the Queen.

Wearing the distinctive purple and gold royal livery, Dettori swept to a thrilling success aboard Enharmonic in the Diomed Stakes. The victory had the royal party, consisting of the Queen, Prince Philip, the Queen Mother and Prince Charles, shouting and gesticulating excitedly as they watched from the stands.

The Queen, who had earlier been presented with a special hand-bound edition of *The Derby* by Tim Neligan and Sir Alastair Burnet, was radiant as she greeted her winner. And as she turned to congratulate Dettori and ply him with the usual technical questions she likes to ask her jockeys, she received the kind of uninhibited response that only Dettori could have produced.

Many young riders faced with the presence of the sovereign on such an auspicious occasion would have been overawed and tongue-tied, but not Frankie. He smiled and chatted away to the Queen of England as if he was talking to his mother back home in his kitchen in Italy.

The trainer of Enharmonic, Lord Huntingdon – whose full name William Edward Robin Hood acknowledges the fact that he is a direct descendant of the legendary hero of Sherwood Forest – says with a degree of amusement: 'Frankie would always be better with a queen than a king. His Latin temperament makes him more suited to a female monarch. He is so totally spontaneous with the Queen, but it is always in a polite way.

'Frankie is a complete professional, but he shows such an obvious enjoyment

Royal seal of approval: The Queen, with her trainer Lord Huntingdon (left) and racing manager Lord Carnarvon (right), greets Enharmonic and Dettori after their victory in the Diomed Stakes at Epsom on Derby day 1993.

of life. One of the best things about him is that even when things go wrong, owners have the feeling that they have got their money's worth.'

Three days after Enharmonic's triumph, Dettori looked very much as if he was on the way to landing his first British classic when he took the lead over quarter of a mile from home in the Oaks aboard Robert Sangster's filly, Oakmead. On the run to the line the tongue-twisting French filly, Intrepidity, proved far too good and Oakmead eventually faded into third place, but as a demonstration of Dettori's growing mastery of the teasing Epsom switchback it was first-class. It was also a harbinger of things to come.

A repeat win on Drum Taps in the Ascot Gold Cup later that month was also carried off with consummate professionalism under the ever-watchful eye of his father, who had walked the course beforehand and advised Frankie where

Pure gold: Dettori savours the heady delight of winning the Ascot Gold Cup on
Drum Taps in 1992 and (right) repeats the feat twelve months later.

the best ground was. 'It was marvellous to watch Frankie on Drum Taps because he rode the horse with such wonderful confidence,' Huntingdon recalls.

The Dettori–Drum Taps partnership moved on to Australia in November where they were strongly fancied to land a historic win in that country's premier event, the Melbourne Cup. They finished only ninth behind Michael Kinane on Vintage Crop, who became the first horse from the northern hemisphere to lift the prize.

July saw Dettori take flight, putting the Hong Kong episode completely behind him. He looked unlucky to be beaten a short head on the Italian-trained Misil – which had been the regular mount of his father before he retired – in the Eclipse Stakes at Sandown, finishing like a train to go down by a whisker to Kinane's mount, Opera House.

Kinane is a quiet, self-effacing man and enjoys his encounters with Dettori at the showcase meetings because he admires the younger man's style. 'I love "scrapping" with Frankie on the racecourse,' says Kinane. 'I don't know him

that well because he's in a different age group, but I think he's great. He's got such a good sense of humour and such an engaging personality. I only wish I was more like him.'

Despite his frustrating defeat in what is one of the most prestigious races in the calendar, Eclipse day proved especially significant for Dettori. He gained his first win on the flying filly, Lochsong, with whom he was to form a unique, crowd-pleasing partnership that illuminated two glorious seasons. He went on to ride her to stunning victories at Goodwood, York and Longchamp in the second half of the season, but we shall look at the Lochsong phenomenon in much greater detail later.

Lochsong apart, winners were beginning to come from all sides and as Dettori booted home doubles, trebles and four-timers he reached sixty-eight for the season by the last week in July, of which an astonishing fifty-two had come since the start of June. Never mind the big money in Hong Kong, he was

OPPOSITE The one that got away: Dettori shows his disappointment after just failing to win the 1993 Eclipse Stakes at Sandown on the Italian-trained Misil, who was beaten inches by Opera House.

RIGHT Taking the Mick: Dettori in typically jokey pose with the brilliant Irish jockey Michael Kinane, who admires the younger man's style.

doing rather nicely in that department back in good old Blighty.

He followed victory on Lochsong in York's Nunthorpe Stakes by lifting two rich prizes at Deauville in August, the Challenge d'Or de Piaget on Prince Babar and the Piaget d'Or on Dana Springs. In the space of forty-eight hours he had scooped prize money of around £500,000, of which his share was approximately £30,000.

'It's the best day's racing I've ever had from a financial point of view,' he said, adding with another little slice of prescience, 'It felt like winning the Breeders' Cup.'

Richard Hannon, the former champion trainer, singles out Dettori's triumph on Dana Springs as one of the most memorable moments of his career. Asked what was so good about it, Hannon replied with typical humour: 'One hundred and eighty thousand pounds!'

Hannon added more seriously: 'That was a great day all round. Frankie rode such a brave race. He took the bull by the horns, jumped out of the stalls and made all the running. He judged it perfectly, they never looked like getting to him.

'Frankie's a big favourite with everyone. Owners particularly like him because he'll stand and talk to them and tell them what went wrong. What more can I say? He's a great jockey, but everybody knows that already.'

In total contrast, the Crowther Homes Handicap at a damp and uninspiring York in October offered only hard slog and modest reward for Dettori, but it showed him in his very best light, giving everything for a relatively small northern trainer, Ernie Weymes, in a way that left the canny Yorkshireman shaking his head in wonder. Riding Weymes's horse, Drummer Hicks, Dettori edged out Pat Eddery on Fox Sparrow by a nostril after a sustained head-to-head duel in the mud that had the crowd as well as Weymes mesmerised.

'Frankie gave my horse an absolutely brilliant ride,' Weymes recalls. 'It was bottomless ground and he was carrying a big weight and there was no way I thought he could win. You don't give those kinds of jockeys instructions, you leave it to them. I just told Frankie that the horse liked to be up with the pace and he was absolutely magnificent. He won by the shortest of short heads and although I was certain he had been beaten, Frankie said he'd definitely won. The irony was that Pat Eddery had ridden Drummer Hicks in his two previous races and didn't get anywhere.'

Weymes, who has been training with considerable success for thirty-seven years, has fond memories of an earlier association with Dettori even though that particular liaison ended in defeat.

'I remember he rode a horse for me at Pontefract one day when he was about eighteen,' Weymes says. 'There were eighteen runners and when Frankie came into the paddock to meet the owners I said to him "Frankie, I'm afraid you've got a bad draw". Frankie said: "I'm a good jockey. I make bad draw good draw". He was as good as his word and he finished third.

'I like Frankie so much, he's such a character. Obviously he doesn't ride for me that much because of his commitments, but he never forgets you. I like to book him whenever I can because he's the best. He's hungry and he always gives everything, unlike a few jockeys I could name. Frankie always rides to the line and past it.'

A week earlier, even Dettori could not overcome the circumstances when he finished a slightly unlucky seventh on Misil in the Prix de l'Arc de Triomphe after his mount lost a shoe and stumbled, but he went on to land the Gran Premio del Jockey Club in Milan on the same horse later that month. However, his momentum was to receive another little jolt when the alleged drugs incident reared its head again and it was announced that he would not be allowed into Japan to ride Misil in the Japan Cup.

An official of the Japan Racing Association was quoted as saying that it was the official policy of the Association not to invite any person who had been involved with drugs. Dettori countered by saying that other riding commitments would have prevented him riding in Japan anyway, and added that he had not applied for a licence to ride in Japan and had not been denied a visa. 'At no time was I charged with any offence,' he reiterated.

There was, however, a flag of truce from the Orient. Dettori rode Marina Park to finish second in the valuable Hong Kong Bowl in December. He had convivial talks with the HK officials and everything was forgotten.

When the 1993 Turf Flat season ended that month, Dettori had notched up a score of 149, his best ever, which was all the more remarkable when you consider that he had managed only fourteen winners by Derby Day at the beginning of June. He finished second in the jockeys' table to Pat Eddery, who amassed 169, but his glow of satisfaction and his immense anticipation of the 1994 season had nothing to do with that winning total.

Back in September something had happened that made Cumani's 'Lucky Lanfranco' tag look, if anything, understated. The sequence of events that led to another extraordinary piece of good fortune for Dettori had begun with the announcement in January that Steve Cauthen had ended his association with Sheikh Mohammed after just over two years as his contracted jockey.

The breakdown in contractual negotiations given as the official reason for the break-up was to a large extent window-dressing. It had been evident to insiders for some while that Cauthen had steadily been losing his appetite for riding and when he announced his retirement from the saddle soon afterwards at the tender age of 32 there were not too many raised eyebrows within the game.

Almost immediately after the revelation of Cauthen's departure, the position of first jockey to the Sheikh was offered to Michael Kinane, again to the surprise of no one. After lengthy negotiations which in terms of their secrecy and intensity rivalled anything NATO might have been involved with, Kinane stunned the racing world by rejecting the Sheikh's overtures.

Kinane's reasoning was reminiscent of the attitude of Cuba's triple Olympic champion boxer, Teofilo Stevenson, who turned down fabulous offers to turn professional in the United States by saying: 'What is a million dollars compared to eight million Cubans who love me?'

Although he was riding out a six-month contract in Hong Kong at the time, Kinane did not want to sever his ties with Ireland and did not like the idea of being constantly apart from his family. He certainly had his priorities right in every sense because with trainers and owners queueing for his services he continued to make frequent sorties from Ireland on the big occasions, lifting major prizes with depressing regularity for his rivals.

The Sheikh's men wasted very little time in pinning down their next quarry, Michael Roberts, who was signed, sealed and delivered by the beginning of February. There was a slight difference between Roberts's contract and

Stevie wonder: Dettori with Steve Cauthen, the American rider who won the
British title three times but quit at the early age of 32.

Cauthen's, however. Thierry Jarnet was to ride the Sheikh's horses trained in
France, which offered a small clue to the logistical difficulties and pressures of
the job that saw Roberts ousted after less than six months.

Roberts had ridden to Group One victories for the Sheikh aboard Opera
House, Intrepidity and Wolfhound that season and was understandably upset.
'Obviously I'm disappointed, but one door closes and another opens,' the
South African said with dignity. 'You can't dwell on these things. It's a difficult
job with the number of horses involved and so many people involved as well.'

The last part of Roberts's statement was the crux of the matter. He had
incurred thirty days' worth of suspensions during the season and things had
simply not been gelling for him the way they had the previous year when he ran
away with the title; but the remark from the Sheikh's racing manager, Anthony

Stroud, to the effect that the decision had been by mutual agreement, said it all. The underlying reason for Roberts's failure to measure up to the task in hand was that it was simply too much fo one man to cope with.

Luca Cumani described it as a job that could crack anybody, and John Gosden, the Sheikh's principal trainer in Britain, said: 'There was no dispute with Michael Roberts. How can anybody sort his way through five or six hundred horses? Often he's at the wrong track, never mind on the wrong horse. Steve Cauthen couldn't manage it and he's the greatest international jockey we've seen for twenty years.'

Even before Roberts admitted defeat there had been rumours circulating that were so compelling in their persistence that it came as no surprise when the whispers were confirmed. Having been vehemently denied by all parties in the best traditions of football management, it was officially announced on 21 September 1993 that Frankie Dettori was to be Sheikh Mohammed's jockey for his horses in training with Gosden.

The men in my life: Sheikh Mohammed (left) and John Gosden, who provided Dettori with the job of a lifetime when it was announced in September 1993 that the young Italian was to be first jockey for the Sheikh's fabulous team of horses trained by Gosden at Newmarket.

The statement that put substance to racing's worst-kept secret said that Michael Roberts's contract would end that year 'as part of a policy decision not to retain one specific jockey for all Darley Stud Management's horses and trainers'. Darley Stud was the umbrella name for the Sheikh's racing operation.

Jarnet was still the Sheikh's jockey in France and the following month it was announced that Kinane would ride for Sheikh Mohammed in major races in 1994, but that did not include the horses trained by Gosden, which were Dettori's exclusive preserve. With impeccable timing Dettori rode the Sheikh's horse Arvola, trained by Gosden, to victory at Nottingham on the day his appointment made the headlines.

So Frankie had done it again: the lucky star was shining more brilliantly than ever. From having appeared to press the self-destruct button, he had made his way to the top of the heap with a peach of a job for the world's most powerful owner that might almost have been tailored to suit his requirements. Had it not been for the drugs allegations he might well have taken up the position in Hong Kong and not been available for the call-up from the Sheikh.

The day Dettori is lost for words bookmakers will start paying out on losing horses, and, beaming broadly as he faced the press, he tossed them a typically colourful line and added a little reminder of his unquenchable ambition for good measure. 'At least I won't have to keep walking around with a smile on my face saying I know nothing!' he said. 'I'm obviously keen to be champion jockey and riding for a stable such as John Gosden's will certainly help my chances.'

The bookies were not that impressed, however. They made Pat Eddery evens favourite for the 1994 championship, with Roberts at 7–4 and Dettori 9–2. For once they were to be caught with the pants of their sharp suits down – but, as they say, more of that later.

Dettori's odds were of no concern to Sheikh Mohammed and his team. They had got their man, although it appeared they had needed to put in a little nifty footwork to catch him. Gosden revealed that they were forced to act quickly because Dettori had also received an offer from the wealthy Parisian art dealer, Daniel Wildenstein, who was the most powerful owner in France after the Aga Khan.

At six feet four inches, with a commanding presence that reminds you more of a statesman or lawyer than a racehorse trainer, Gosden is not the kind of man you ignore easily. He is the son of the renowned trainer 'Towser' Gosden, who made innumerable successful raids on the bookmakers' coffers from his lair in Lewes, Sussex.

Gosden completed his university education and, eschewing his father's advice ('Whatever you do don't be a trainer'), went to work for arguably the two greatest post-war trainers, Sir Noel Murless and Vincent O'Brien, before moving to California where he started up on his own with just three horses in 1979.

Having proved himself up with the best in the States, where his career was highlighted by the victory of Robert Sangster's Royal Heroine in the Breeders' Cup Mile, Gosden was head-hunted by Sheikh Mohammed and brought over to train for him in 1988 at the historic Stanley House stables built by the 16th Earl of Derby eighty-five years earlier.

Gosden, whose wife Rachel is a barrister, is a man who brings a thoughtful yet light-hearted approach to the sport that Phil Bull, the erudite founder of racing's 'bible' *Timeform*, described so memorably as 'the great triviality'.

Looking back on his part in the decision to sign Dettori, Gosden says the Italian was in his estimation the obvious choice. 'I had first come across Frankie when I was training in the States,' Gosden recalls. 'He got on well with the jockeys out there and learnt a good deal. He always came across as a very positive, helpful fellow.

'When it was decided that it was not practicable to have one jockey for all the Sheikh's horses and that they would have a stable jockey instead I was asked for my opinion. It was obvious to me that Frankie was the right young talent and it made sense to link up with an up-and-coming star.

'I remember years ago when Stavros Niarchos was looking for a jockey I went through the list with Philip Payne-Gallwey, his racing manager. The one that was obvious to me was Cash Asmussen because he was just coming up in the States. You want to look for an accomplished jockey, but one who is still ascending.'

There were many qualities in Dettori that appealed to Gosden. Looking at the technical side first, Gosden summarises the Italian's horsemanship by saying: 'Frankie is the most brilliant young talent we have. He combines the American and European styles so effectively. He has a crouched position, but it is not overstated. He rides with his toe in the stirrup and changes hands on a horse in a flamboyant manner, which is something he learnt from Chris McCarron in the States.

'He gets a good deal of the run out of the horse before he has to resort to the stick. Many jockeys over here don't do that. He has excellent balance and keeps horses on an even keel. He gives horses great confidence through a race and has superb hands. Horses come back well after Frankie rides them.'

Having reiterated that the position was untenable when one jockey was being asked to ride all the Sheikh's horses, Gosden says: 'The system works far better now with Kinane and Jarnet there as well. I make sure to plan well ahead so Frankie knows what track he's going to. I try to send him to big tracks to enable him to fulfil his career. I wouldn't want to see the arrangement with the stable get in the way.'

Being able to ride well is only part of the equation with a pressure job like the Sheikh's which still demands the highest level of commitment and application despite the revised format. Gosden chose Dettori as much because he considered he had the right mental attitude for the job. He saw behind the sometimes brash, extrovert image and discerned a young man with maturity beyond his years.

'What people do not realise about Frankie is that behind the happy-go-lucky exuberant exterior lurks a very sharp mind,' says Gosden. 'He's a real thinker and thinks well ahead. He has an opinion on every horse, though of course he's not always right. He is very single-minded, but he's also totally up-front and straight.

'Being a jockey is so demanding with the relentless schedules and having to watch your weight all the time. But Frankie has such a positive attitude and it goes through to the horse and the racing public. His character comes through in his riding, he can express himself through it.

'When he had the problem with Hong Kong it was all coming too easy and it could have been the undoing of anyone else. But Frankie turned the whole thing round and made it a positive influence on his life.'

Indeed he did, to such an extent that he found himself in a position that even he, for all his innate self-belief, would have found hard to imagine just a few months previously. Being number one for Gosden provided the perfect base from which to launch a challenge for the jockey's title he wanted so badly.

Success breeds success in racing's fickle world and all that needed to happen was for Gosden to turn out a regular supply of winners from his 180-horse yard to set the machine in motion and have other trainers and owners falling over themselves to get in on the Dettori show – that is if they weren't already.

But success can sometimes be hollow if, behind the backslapping and the celebrations, there is an emotional void that demands to be filled. That was still very much the case with Dettori as his star rose ever higher. He could be champion jockey a thousand times over but there would always be a sense that something was missing until he put things right with the man who had guided him, supported him and nurtured him throughout those turbulent, formative years of his career.

To say that Dettori's spurning of Cumani was like an open wound would not be exaggerating the pain. At the very moment he was being hailed as the heir apparent to the Flat-race crown, feelings of loss, remorse, and just a good old-fashioned need to make things right were eating away at the young Italian.

Eventually it became too much to bear. Pride is often strongest in a young heart, but shortly before the formal announcement of his link-up with Sheikh Mohammed, Dettori decided humility was the only course to follow and made what must have been the most difficult journey of his life.

Towards the end of August, almost eight months after Cumani had sent him packing, with what he now accepted was good reason, Dettori showed up at Cumani's yard determined to end the bad blood between them. His reception was not so much frosty as wet.

'Frankie came round one evening in late August.' Cumani recalls. 'It was pouring down with rain and he knocked at the door of my office and said "Can I come in?" I was doing my paperwork and I remained sitting at my desk and said "No, you can stay outside and get soaking wet. Then you can come in."

'So he stood there and got soaked through. Eventually I said "Okay, you can come in now". He came inside absolutely dripping, we both laughed and then we had a drink and started talking. Frankie apologised over the Hong Kong business and the whole thing was forgotten.'

There was, however, one proviso to Cumani's willingness to forgive and forget. 'I had said I wouldn't give him a ride on one of my horses for a year and I stuck to it,' says Cumani. 'He didn't ride for me again until the following June at Royal Ascot when I put him up on Relatively Special in the Coronation Stakes, which unfortunately was a loser.'

Dettori wouldn't have minded if he had ended up riding the worst horse in the yard round lowly Southwell on a freezing cold winter's evening. His worst fears had been allayed: Cumani had been prepared to wipe out the past and everything was hunky-dory again in what was possibly the most important relationship in his life outside of his family. In some ways that was almost worth more than all the riches that might come his way from Sheikh Mohammed.

Chapter Five
The Lochsong Monster

Racing's so-called 'glorious uncertainty' derails the best-laid plans almost on a daily basis, but 1994 proved to be everything that Frankie Dettori could have hoped for and a lot more besides. At the still tender age of 23 everything came together in a way that even he could not have anticipated the previous autumn when he signed up for Sheikh Mohammed and declared himself in hot pursuit of Pat Eddery's crown.

The transition from prince of the track to king was never just a case of an outstanding young rider fulfilling his potential and becoming champion jockey. The phenomenon that is Frankie Dettori superstar involves a lot more than winning a sackful of races. Dettori not only captivated the racing world but transcended it, too. It was his charisma and his showmanship that launched the Dettori story into orbit at least as much as his riding.

Besides his talent and his special brand of *chutzpah*, there was one particular ingredient that helped Dettori touch the hearts and minds of the racing public in a very special way as he gradually took on the mantle of the people's champion. As a healthy, young Latin male he had doubtless run his eye over more than a few alluring females in his time, but he had never seen anything like the one that shimmied into his life in the spring of 1993.

Dettori's partnership with the flying filly, Lochsong, spun a golden thread through two glorious seasons. The irrepressible Italian and the imperious queen of speed were made for each other and in terms of scene stealing they upstaged classic winners and champions of the European circuit on a regular basis. So, before looking at Dettori's *annus mirabilis* in detail, let us first chart the course of the whirlwind romance that became part of racing folklore.

In July 1994, I wrote in the *Sunday Times*: 'Racing has become obsessed with middle-distance excellence and the most exciting attribute of the thoroughbred is in danger of being relegated to relative insignificance. Sheer, blinding speed is still one of the most exhilarating sights you can see on a racecourse, and watching Lochsong produce that amazing after-burner thrust to kill off the opposition in a few explosive strides can take the breath away.'

While it was Lochsong's extraordinary acceleration that entranced racing *aficionados,* there was another reason why she established herself as one of the most popular horses of the past two or three decades. In an era when many top horses are whisked off to stud at the end of their three-year-old careers, Lochsong raced until she was six before retiring to her owner, Jeff Smith's, Littleton Stud in Hampshire at the end of the 1994 campaign. She was therefore able to build a unique rapport with her legion of admirers.

The other crucial factor in Lochsong's public persona was her partnership with Dettori. It may sound faintly silly to compare the characters of a horse and a man, but Lochsong and Dettori were in a sense kindred spirits, both possessing an innate brilliance and a theatrical flair, tempered by a streak of stubborn independence which often characterises great performers.

Lord John Oaksey, the writer and broadcaster, who wrote the script for the official video of Lochsong's career, described them as 'twin souls', and Ian Balding, the horse's trainer, says: 'It was a partnership made in heaven. You don't get many Flat horses who race as much as Lochsong did, which is what helped to endear her to the public. But Frankie was very much part of what made Lochsong so popular.'

Dettori was still a struggling apprentice when Lochsong was born at Smith's picturesque stud three miles outside Chichester in 1988. Their paths were not to cross for another five years and in the intervening period the feisty female would have several partners before settling down with the young man who would guide her to her most glittering triumphs.

Smith, who is Chairman and Chief Executive of AIM Group plc which makes interiors for aircraft, is considered one of the luckiest owners in racing. He bought his first horse, Rush Bond, in 1976 for just £1,200 and it won him three races. His best horses before Lochsong were the brilliant miler, Chief Singer, and the precociously talented two-year-old, Dashing Blade.

Away from the pressures of his business, racing was Smith's great passion, but it was the breeding side that particularly fascinated him, and in 1984 he purchased the 190-acre Littleton Stud, where Lochsong's sire, Song, was the resident stallion. Song was the champion sprinter of 1969, but he was temperamental and passed his cussedness on to many of his progeny.

The idea of mating Song with an almost equally stroppy mare in the speedy but inconsistent Peckitts Well, who Smith purchased at the Newmarket December sales, might have seemed destined to produce a moody monster of a horse. But Smith knew his bloodlines and perhaps he was subconsciously indulging in a little reverse psychology on the basis that breeding's basic theory of like begetting like very rarely works out.

The first sign that Lochsong might prove something of a handful to train came early in her career when she was sent to the Newmarket yard of Lord John FitzGerald, who had achieved considerable success with previous progeny of Song. However, it was not Lochsong's mental state that frustrated

ABOVE Splendour in the grass: Lochsong (left) relaxes at owner Jeff Smith's picturesque Hampshire stud where she was born. RIGHT What do you think, Frankie? Jeff Smith talking with Dettori at York in 1993.

FitzGerald, but seemingly insuperable physical problems that prohibited him from training her.

So Lochsong went back to Smith's stud for a year and was then sent to Balding at Kingsclere with the instruction from her owner 'Try to win a little race with her and then we'll retire her'. Balding recalls: 'She was big, gawky and very unsound when she came to me. She had very bad joints and knees and used to trot like a cripple.'

Nevertheless, Balding managed to get her on to a course in July 1991, and after finishing second at Salisbury she won a small race at Redcar ridden by Ray Cochrane. Balding assumed that as she had done the job she would be retired, but with Smith out of the country, he managed to obtain the permission of Smith's racing manager, Ron Sheather, to run her in an apprentice race at Newbury where she was ridden to the narrowest of victories by Francis 'Scully' Arrowsmith, the stable's claiming rider.

Realising that she had such a tremendous will to race, Smith decided to keep Lochsong in training as a four-year-old. She showed stunning improvement and formed a partnership with Willie Carson that brought off the first two legs of an unprecedented big-race treble.

Blazing the trail from the start, in a manner that was to become her most

famous characteristic, Lochsong raced to victories in the Stewards' Cup at Goodwood and Portland Handicap at Doncaster and became the first horse to win those two races and the Ayr Gold Cup in the same season when she annihilated the opposition in the Scottish event.

With Carson unavailable, Lochsong was ridden at Ayr by the capable Arrowsmith, who took a leaf out of Dettori's book by punching the air as he passed the post. Perhaps part of Arrowsmith's pleasure, and Smith's too, was cocking a snook at Channel 4's betting guru, John McCririck. In typically brash fashion, McCririck referred to Lochsong's apparently unfavourable high draw and told viewers 'Lochsong *will not* win'. As a consequence, Smith helped himself to what were unexpectedly generous odds.

Smith and Balding set their sights on a far more ambitious programme in 1993, forsaking the lucrative but limiting handicap scene for the opportunity to prove Lochsong a championship contender by taking on the best sprinters at level weights in the more prestigious listed and pattern races. Three lacklustre defeats in the hands of three different jockeys in the opening weeks of the 1993 season left her connections scratching their heads. But, although they could not possibly have realised it, the first seeds of the dream team had already been sewn.

Having been ridden by Carson and Piggott in those first two inglorious defeats at Newmarket and York, Lochsong came home an undistinguished fourth behind her old rival, Paris House, in the Temple Stakes at Sandown. As far as formbook experts and indeed Smith and Balding were concerned, it seemed that her best days might already be behind her.

They had reckoned without the young man on her back at Sandown. Dettori, who rode her for the first time there, was possessed of the same resilience as Lochsong and he, too, had just fallen heavily from grace. The empathy between them not only rekindled her competitive flame, but turned it into a raging furnace that lit up the racetracks of Europe and also played a significant part in sending Dettori's once-flagging career into orbit.

Dettori was chosen to replace Carson as Lochsong's rider principally because the Scot was becoming more and more difficult to pin down. 'We felt we could lose Willie because there was always the possibility he might be claimed to ride for Hamdan al Maktoum, as was the case in the July Cup in 1993,' explains Smith. 'Frankie had gone freelance at that time and of all the freelances we felt he was the best. We felt that if we stuck with him we would always get him.'

Dettori certainly needed people to stand by him at that point because without the support of leading trainers and owners he could very quickly have been on a downhill slope. One of the men who provided him with just the type of backing he needed was Balding, who took to Frankie in a major way, both as a rider and a person.

A former leading amateur rider, Cambridge Rugby Blue and all-round sportsman of note, the affable Balding has prepared a clutch of outstanding horses at his historic Kingsclere yard, where John Porter trained seven Derby winners. Balding produced another, the mighty Mill Reef, who added victories in the Eclipse Stakes, King George VI and Queen Elizabeth Diamond Stakes and Prix de l'Arc de Triomphe to his success in the 1971 Derby. A bronze statue of Mill Reef now stands majestically in the stable yard.

Balding's list of patrons reads like a Who's Who of the Turf and, besides Smith, includes the Queen, Mill Reef's owner Paul Mellon and Sheikh Mohammed. In his lengthy career he has used just about every top British-based rider of the past three decades and he puts Dettori right up with the very best.

'I think Frankie's the most exciting talent since Lester Piggott as a youngster,' Balding says. 'But he's more flamboyant than Lester and he's more disciplined in a race. He's the best thing to happen to racing for a long time.'

During 1993, Balding provided Dettori with thirty winners, which played an invaluable part in his resurgence. 'After he completed a four-timer at Newbury, including two of ours, Tissisat and Winged Victory, he rode for us regularly,' recalls Balding. 'I think he really appreciated it because we gave him a chance at a time in his career when he needed it.'

On a personal level, Balding's relationship with Dettori did not match his closeness with Cumani because Dettori rode for Balding only on a freelance basis. However, Balding says that Dettori became very much one of the family, getting on particularly well with his son and daughter, Andrew and Clare, and his wife Emma.

There is a large picture of Frankie occupying pride of place in the Baldings' kitchen, almost diagonally opposite a portrait of Piggott in Balding's study. Bring up the subject of Dettori and the entire Balding family will respond enthusiastically, each contributing their own personal tribute plus a fund of stories, amusing and otherwise.

Clare, who is now a successful journalist and broadcaster on radio and television, remembers that when Dettori first came to stay at Kingsclere his reputation suffered a knock, but it had nothing to do with horses: 'The first time Frankie stayed here, Uncle Willie [Lord Huntingdon] told him to lock his bedroom door because I was a nymphomaniac! I don't know if he did lock it, but he certainly looked very worried and he didn't come out all night!'

Having destroyed Dettori's ladykiller image, Clare adds: 'Frankie's just like one of the family when he stays. He raids the fridge all the time – he had a whole half chicken once. Now that I'm on Radio One he always says "Hey Clare, 'ow's Chris Evans?" whenever he sees me at the races. The wonderful thing about Frankie is that he has no arrogance at all, which is amazing considering what he's achieved.'

Andrew recalls another episode the first time Dettori stayed at Kingsclere. 'Whenever anyone comes here Dad has to show them the Mill Reef film and bore them to death. But Frankie was sitting on the edge of the chair, saying "Let's see that bit again". It didn't matter that it was getting quite late and he had six booked rides the next day.'

As well as being assistant to his uncle Toby, who is also a leading trainer, Andrew is a successful amateur rider like his sister, and it is Dettori's professionalism that captivates him most. 'Dad is quite funny about his jockeys, but he adores Frankie,' Andrew says. 'I think he rides the way Dad would if he rode professionally. They think similarly.

'Frankie's genuinely gutted if he gets beaten and you can tell him "You got that wrong" and he accepts it. Some jockeys come here and get off the horses and don't say anything. Frankie always has something to contribute.

'He's always thinking about horses and the way to ride them. After he'd ridden a horse called Stiletto Blade he rang up and said "I was thinking about Stiletto Blade. Maybe he should do this next time". With Lochsong he'd ring up every week and say "Perhaps we should do this or that".'

The first time he rode Lochsong in public, Dettori was the one on the receiving end of all the advice. 'When Frankie finished fourth on the horse in the Temple Stakes he told me afterwards that everyone had told him to do something different and in the end he didn't know what to do,' Balding explains.

Dettori elaborated by saying: 'When I was asked to ride her at Sandown, I talked to Willie Carson, Lester Piggott, Jeff Smith and Ron Sheather and they all told me something different. One said "Try to lead", somebody else said "Try to save a bit". I was a little bit confused. I wasn't really sure what I was doing. My first ride on her wasn't my best one.'

Their next outing together went far more smoothly when Lochsong skated home in the Advanced Micro Devices Sprint at Sandown, making all the running and coming home a long way ahead of Bunty Boo. Frankie still wasn't sure he had got the hang of her, however, and once again he found he was bemused by conflicting orders when she had her next race, in the King George Stakes at Goodwood. This time, however, he did it his way as she held off Paris House after a head-to-head tussle.

'It was very foggy that day and nobody could see a thing, so I thought: sod my orders, I'll do my own thing', he explained. 'I just threw the reins at her and let her do whatever she wanted. After she won everyone said "Oh, you rode the perfect race, you saved a bit for the end". But I didn't do a thing. I just let her do her own thing. That race was vital to me.'

Frankie had finally discovered this was one female who would not be dominated and he had that fact underlined when he rode her in a workout not long afterwards. The tranquil splendour of Balding's breathtaking Valley gallop has seen many a brilliant workout by a whole host of champions, but Lochsong had never been one to perform to order at home and on this particular morning the carefully orchestrated pipe-opener degenerated into farce.

'Frankie was supposed to hold her back behind Poker Chip,' Balding recalls. 'But he couldn't hold her and she zigzagged all over the place. I said to him "What on earth were you doing?" and he tried to make a joke of it, saying "She wants more than six furlongs, doesn't she?".'

Once again the shortcomings of her home work meant nothing. Lochsong's

Getting it together: Dettori gains the first of many memorable victories on Lochsong in Sandown's Advanced Micro Devices Sprint in 1993.

Doing it her way: Dettori soon realised that the best way to ride Lochsong was to let her do whatever she wanted and he ignored his orders when riding her to victory in Goodwood's King George Stakes in 1993.

Duchess of York: Lochsong puts a field of high-class sprinters in their place in the 1993 Nunthorpe Stakes at York.

next race, the Nunthorpe Stakes at York, showed her to be well in line for the title of champion sprinter. This time she held off Paris House far more easily than she had at Goodwood with a quality field trailing behind.

The Nunthorpe was significant not only for a superb performance by Lochsong. It was the first occasion that Dettori's uninhibited displays of elation became almost as memorable as the victory itself. There was a huge grin of triumph and a finger raised in the air to denote number one as he passed the post. Then, as he returned to the winner's enclosure he clenched his fist and shouted exultantly 'Yes!'.

But the best was saved for after he had dismounted. Dettori's command of English though by now fairly comprehensive was still not perfect by any means. But one thing he never lacked was a turn of phrase and the ability to produce a quotable quote. Referring to Lochsong's amazing speed he said: 'She's like Linford Christie without the lunchbox.'

On a more serious note, Dettori then explained how he had developed the knack of riding this complex racehorse to maximum effect. 'I try to sit motionless on her because she is so exceptional,' he said. 'She is very different from other sprinters you ride. They get on their toes. She realised she had to relax halfway and have a breather. She's more mature now.'

The honeymoon came to a temporary halt at Haydock, where Lochsong showed that six furlongs was not her optimum distance and finished only third to Wolfhound and Catrail. Putting that little blip behind her, she went next to Paris on 'Arc day' at the beginning of October and won in a manner that clinched not only the title of champion sprinter, but Racehorse of the Year as well.

Though she was tackling the best in Europe in the Prix de l'Abbaye de Longchamp, it wasn't so much a competitive event as a slaughter. It was a performance that above all others stamped her as the horse of a lifetime.

As the crowds streamed out through the gates at Longchamp into the hurly-burly of a Paris evening at the end of an extraordinary Arc de Triomphe day, the talk was not so much of the French filly, Urban Sea, who had belied her long odds to win the premier middle-distance event of Europe, but of another remarkable female talent. Even the most experienced racegoers could not recall anything quite like Lochsong's breathtaking brilliance in the Abbaye.

As a race it was a non-event. Catapulting out of the gate, Lochsong had run the supposedly top-class opposition off their feet after two furlongs. After three furlongs she already had the rest in such desperate trouble as she blazed further and further ahead that you wondered if she had gone too fast and would pay the penalty in the later stages.

In the end Lochsong sailed home almost the length of the Champs Elysées in front of Stack Rock, with Dettori wondering whether some over-zealous fan of Lochsong had gone to work on the rest with a shotgun. Looking elated but almost disbelieving, he commented: 'I have ridden many good horses, but I've never been as fast as that in my life. All I heard during the race was the wind whistling past my ears.'

One expert could hardly believe his eyes, or more significantly his watch, as he logged Lochsong's show of sustained gate-to-wire acceleration. Michael Tanner, Britain's foremost authority on sectional timing, said afterwards: 'People always talk about Lochsong being so electric from the gate and she is. But when she won the Abbaye her final furlong was so fast that I began to wonder if there had been a malfunction in the timing system.'

The official breakdown showed that Lochsong's times for the individual metric furlongs were 13.1, 13.1, 11.2, 11.4 and 10.9 seconds. The final furlongs of the previous five Abbayes were 11.1, 12.1, 12.0, 13.0 and 12.5 seconds. Her last three furlongs put even the brilliant Dayjur's winning run in the 1990 Abbaye in the shade and he was racing on faster ground.

'In my experience, no sprint is ever likely to be concluded by the fastest furlong of the race, let alone one breaking 11 seconds on heavy ground,' Tanner said.

So, Europe had a speed queen the likes of whom few if any could ever recall seeing. And the marvellous thing from racing's point of view was that Smith was intent on keeping her in training as long as she maintained her enthusiasm and her blistering pace.

Any doubts on that score were soon dispelled with interest when she returned to the track for her first race as a six-year-old at the beginning of the 1994 season. Balding had made no secret of the fact that he did not consider her completely ready for her comeback event, the Palace House Stakes at Newmarket, describing her as only 80 per cent fit.

The mind boggled as to what she would have done if she had been 100 per cent fit; Tanner would definitely have been asking for the timing system to be checked. Lochsong once again, to use that oldest of racing clichés, turned the race into a procession. Sauntering home in a way that must have made Dettori

Poleaxed in Paris: Lochsong leaves the crowds gasping in disbelief as she turns in a stunning display of acceleration to win the 1993 Prix de l'Abbaye de Longchamp by a wide margin.

almost embarrassed to draw his riding fee, Lochsong broke the track record by over half a second.

The roadshow rolled on to Sandown Park with Lochsong delighting the vast crowd with a facile victory over Lavinia Fontana in the Temple Stakes, the race in which her partnership with Dettori had got off to such a forgettable start twelve months previously. What a difference a year made. The unsaddling enclosure was a seething mass of people inside and out and as the partnership returned they were treated to the kind of wild acclaim that had once been reserved for the great Desert Orchid after his many emotional triumphs there.

Like 'Dessie', Lochsong was receiving fan mail by the truck load at this stage, with huge numbers of packets of Polo mints arriving for her at Balding's yard. Even the normally low-key Balding was caught up in the euphoria and ready to trot out the superlatives, as I discovered on a visit to Kingsclere during the run-up to her next race, the King's Stand Stakes at Royal Ascot.

'She's the fastest horse I've ever had anything to do with and that includes Mill Reef,' he said. 'She's just phenomenal and I really believe she's better than ever this year. She's twenty kilos heavier and has a lot more muscle.

'She's much easier to train, too. She swims a lot and she basically gets herself fit and does her own thing. We rarely gallop her with another horse because there is nothing fast enough to go with her. Like most sprinters, she wants to get everything over with as quickly as possible and then she stands and watches the rest gallop.'

After that visit I suggested in an article in the *Sunday Times* that, if Lochsong were a woman, Emma Balding would have serious grounds for concern. As the master of Park House Stables lovingly ran his experienced hands over the finer aspects of Lochsong's magnificent frame, he was quite clearly besotted.

'Just look at that bottom,' he said, pointing to her prodigiously muscled backside. 'She didn't have that last year. And she didn't have a neck like that either.'

Lochsong was posturing blatantly in her box like some equine catwalk queen, although infinitely more refined, and she obviously revelled in the attention. 'She loves the camera and she poses straight away,' Balding said. 'Although she can be a funny old character at times, she has a lovely temperament, although she might take a bite at you if you happened to catch her at the wrong moment.'

Fast-moving females have been the downfall of many a blinkered fellow, but when Lochsong cantered down to the start for the King's Stand Stakes she represented a glorious certainty for punters and *aficionados* alike. She didn't let them down, streaking ahead of the pack of predatory males who were limited to a distant view of that elegant backside disappearing ever further into the distance.

Having been almost motionless throughout the race, Dettori more than

Easy pickings: Lochsong cruises home well ahead of the chasing pack to win the 1994
King's Stand Stakes at Royal Ascot.

made up for it in the winner's enclosure. After his now obligatory punch in the
air, he kissed Lochsong on the nose and gave Balding a slap on the back that
almost floored him.

Smith was already talking about keeping Lochsong in training as a seven-
year-old, something virtually unheard of for a Flat horse of her class. We
wondered if there would ever be an end to this fabulous piece of racing theatre

and although we could never have realised it at that stage, the answer – or at least the first clue – was shortly to reveal itself.

With Dettori claimed to ride Catrail for Sheikh Mohammed, Willie Carson was recalled to action for Lochsong's next race, the July Cup at Newmarket. Everything was set for another queenly display. The car parks at the July course were full to overflowing, but Lochsong's legions of fans left the track with heavy hearts and, in many cases, lighter wallets too.

The first broad hint that this was not to be just another victory parade came long before Lochsong entered the stalls. Showing the first real public sign of the temperament that had afflicted both her parents, she took off with Carson on the way to the start and, as he struggled to hold her, much of the crackling energy that she would normally have used to burn off the opposition was dissipated.

Doubtless mindful of the pre-race shenanigans, Carson partially restrained Lochsong in the early part of the race and although she took her customary lead she was never dominating in her usual style. She was in trouble fully two furlongs from the finish and was passed by all but one of her eight rivals on the run to the line.

Some had expressed doubts before the race about whether Lochsong would be as effective on her return to six furlongs, but in truth she would not have won over five that day. Most observers tended to point the finger at Carson, including Dettori, whose immediate reaction was to say 'He should have let her go'.

According to Balding that was purely a heat-of-the-moment thing because Dettori (who had finished third on Catrail) was distressed by her defeat. On reflection, he would doubtless have shared Balding's view that no blame could be attached to Carson. 'You always tend to say that because it's six furlongs you've got to keep a bit up your sleeve,' Balding reflects. 'You cannot blame Willie. She'd done too much going down to the start and he'd done well to stop her.'

Any worries about her enthusiasm or her temperament were assuaged, temporarily at least, when Dettori rode her to a clear-cut but hard-fought success over Mistertopogigo in Goodwood's King George Stakes three weeks later. It wasn't foggy, as it had been twelve months previously when she won; this time it was pouring with rain. Nothing could dampen Dettori's joy at being reunited with his queen, however. He kissed her on the mouth and said: 'She's the fastest thing on earth!'

So, it was on to a repeat attempt in the Nunthorpe Stakes at York the following month. Any similarities to the previous year were impossible to detect and, to the despair of her connections and perhaps a degree of justifiable *schadenfreude* from Carson, Lochsong showed that she could be as difficult as any human prima donna. She completely blew her top in the preliminaries and finished last (Dettori eased right off when she was beaten) behind Smith's other runner, Blue Siren, also trained by Balding.

96

Trevor Jones

Top of the world: Dettori roars his delight as he passes the post on Barathea to win the 1994 Breeders' Cup Mile at Churchill Downs.

ABOVE AND LEFT Man about the house: Dettori's hectic schedule allows him little time for normal domestic routine, but here he is seen in less pressured circumstances at his home in Newmarket.

OPPOSITE Doubly Glorious Goodwood: Dettori rides Lochsong to victory in the King George Stakes at Goodwood in 1993 (top) and 1994.

Trevor Jones

Trevor Jones

ABOVE Command performance: Dettori initiates a Royal Ascot treble on the Queen's filly Phantom Gold in the 1995 Ribblesdale Stakes. He had been a hot favourite to win the Ritz Club Trophy but finished one winner behind Michael Kinane.

OPPOSITE Walter's revenge: Dettori wins the Oaks for the second year running on Moonshell (top), beating Walter Swinburn on Dance A Dream. Twenty-four hours later, riding Tamure in the Derby, he is collared in the shadow of the post by Swinburn on Lammtarra (green colours).

LEFT Dettori (left) in relaxed mood with Luca Cumani on the Newmarket gallops. The relationship between the two men was stretched to breaking point when Dettori sought to pursue the glamour and riches of Hong Kong in 1993, but they got together again the following year to bring off their greatest triumph in the Breeders' Cup.

BELOW Dream team: Dettori raises his whip in jubilation as he wins the 1994 Irish Derby on the brilliant filly Balanchine.

Trevor Jones

George Selwyn

My hero: Sheikh Mohammed allows his feelings to take over as he celebrates
Balanchine's Irish Derby triumph with Dettori.

Gerry Cranham

RIGHT Dettori enjoys one of his easiest victories in a Group One race as he coasts home on Only Royale to win the Yorkshire Oaks at York in 1994.

BELOW What's in a name? Dettori and Vettori win the 1995 French 2,000 Guineas at Longchamp.

John Crofts

John Crofts

Lochsong crashed into the gate on the way out on to the track and then took off. 'As soon as she got on to the track she was like a lunatic,' Dettori recalled. 'After the long lead-up and all the media attention she just flipped. It wasn't her fault, she's just an animal. But she's a very fit animal and when she got to the start she wasn't blowing too hard and had plenty of time to walk round. Obviously she just wasn't herself in the race.'

Smith blamed the pre-race parade, but Balding is not convinced it was the parade that was the cause, as was generally assumed afterwards. 'I don't think she was right. I think she had a touch of something,' he says. 'I think whatever she'd have done she'd have cleared off with Frankie on the way to the start.'

With a cruel twist of the knife, the York stewards added to the pain Smith

Throwing it all away: An overwrought Lochsong bolts to post before the 1994 Nunthorpe Stakes at York. Her pre-race antics saw her finish at the back of the field, as she had done in Newmarket's July Cup the previous month.

Queen of Europe: Lochsong races to a repeat success in the Prix de l'Abbaye at Longchamp in 1994, dispelling fears that her temperament had finally got the better of her.

and Balding were feeling by disqualifying Blue Siren from first place and awarding the race to Piccolo. Smith was so devastated by the Lochsong débâcle that he hardly noticed.

'It seems extraordinary that I felt no euphoria after winning a Group One race with a home-bred filly,' he says. 'But my emotions were totally flat. I had no interest in it. I didn't really take in the fact that Blue Siren had been disqualified.'

If it was possible, Dettori was even more shattered than Smith. 'I don't think I've ever seen a jockey feel so badly about a defeat,' Smith recalls. 'He was really upset for her as well as himself. There was great affection between them. The whole thing was a disaster; he felt circumstances had conspired against her. It's the only time I've seen Frankie really shocked by events. It was the way it happened.'

Dettori added a postscript to the York débâcle that was both amusing and poignant. 'I talk to her in English because she's English,' he said. 'The only time I talked to her in Italian was after York. We tried to blame her for that and make out she was a beast. But she's not a beast – she's like one of us.'

There was now a real question-mark over Lochsong's future. She was taken back to Smith's stud with her nerves in a terrible state. Everyone feared that her temperament had irrevocably worsened, but she calmed down in the therapeutic Hampshire air to such an extent that Balding not only got her back on track for a second crack at the Prix de l'Abbaye, but sent her over to Longchamp with a high degree of confidence as well.

On that first Sunday in October 1994, the huge British contingent were to suffer yet another sickening blow in the main event, the Prix de l'Arc de Triomphe, with the eclipse of all five British runners behind Sheikh Mohammed's Carnegie. But, just as it had been twelve months earlier, the pain was eased considerably through another stunning triumph by Lochsong.

The French authorities were extremely sympathetic to Balding's worries over the preliminaries and allowed Lochsong to do just a quick turn in the paddock and take a long, slow walk to the start before the other runners had even filed out on to the course. They needn't have bothered coming out at all. Lochsong was almost as far in front of them in the race, coming home five lengths clear of Mistertopogigo in a time that was two and a half seconds faster than the previous year when the ground had been far more testing.

'That second Abbaye win was very special because everyone, including me, felt that she might have gone over the top temperamentally,' Balding said. 'But she proved us wrong completely.'

This time the celebrations went right off the end of the Richter scale. Even the French joined in the tumultuous ovation for a spectacular partnership. And, just as you would have expected, Dettori responded in the only way he knows how. This time, though, he even excelled himself with his display of pure uninhibited showmanship.

Having shown us a new party piece, a double clenched-fist salute, as he entered the famous tree-lined winner's circle, Dettori then shouted 'Monster' as he dismounted, tossed his goggles into the crowd, set off on a round of high-fives with everyone in sight and then did a lap of honour holding his sporting print trophy above his head.

But the most extravagent gesture was reserved for Jeff Smith, or 'Jeffsmiff' as Dettori calls him. As Balding stood there in tears, Dettori gave the solidly built Smith a bearhug and tried – almost successfully – to lift him right off the ground. For a man of Frankie's diminutive proportions this was a pretty brave thing to attempt. By comparison, Balding's hug was a relatively simple, feet-on-the-ground affair.

'He's such an ebullient character. He wears his heart on his sleeve and it's so infectious,' says Smith. 'His actions are so totally spontaneous and that's what made it so good.'

Balding echoes that view, saying: 'He's got such terrific character, that guy, he plays the emotions of everyone. He was terribly excited and relieved and

Party time in Paris: Dettori begins a round of frenzied celebrations as he returns
triumphant to the winner's enclosure at Longchamp.

thrilled like all of us. But in his Latin way he showed it rather better.'

Dettori admitted he milked the emotional high for all it was worth. 'I had
experienced it the previous year and I knew the Brits were in love with her, so I
took full advantage of it and made a show out of it,' he said. 'But it was true
feelings, something I'll never forget. It was like scoring a goal at Wembley for
your favourite club.'

Dettori had shown his affection for Lochsong when he rested his head on her
neck and patted her fondly. In a typically evocative way, he summarised what
she meant to racing fans and to him personally:

100

'People love to see a horse like her, running from the front, ears pricked, no dangers,' he said. 'She's my favourite and the people's favourite because of the way she races.'

With Lochsong apparently right back to her best it was decided to aim for the biggest pot of the lot. Smith had long harboured a dream of sending her to America for the Breeders' Cup Sprint and she was dispatched to Churchill Downs in Louisville, Kentucky, in November for the $1 million contest that traditionally begins the seven-race programme.

While one firm of British bookmakers installed Lochsong as 7–2 favourite for the Kentucky event, there were those who made predictions of doom and gloom as she winged her way across the Atlantic. It was not so much because the doubters feared she might boil over in the pressure cooker atmosphere of international racing's most celebrated occasion, rather that her task against the American flyers over six furlongs on an unfamiliar dirt surface appeared to be bordering on the impossible.

British raiders had fared poorly in the eleven previous runnings of the Breeders' Cup it was true, but two outstanding British sprinters, Dayjur and Sheikh Albadou, had shown that it was possible to beat the stateside speedsters at their own game.

Dayjur had been the moral winner of the 1990 Sprint in New York. He had the race at his mercy, but jumped a dark shadow some fifty yards from the line, and another just before the wire, and thereby forfeited the prize. Sheikh Albadou annihilated the locals the following year when the race was run over the same Churchill Downs track where Lochsong was set to strut her stuff in 1994.

Any doubts the Americans had about Lochsong being in the same league as that pair were dispelled on the run-up to the race in the most astonishing manner. Two days before the Breeders' Cup, Dettori and Lochsong caused pandemonium among the media correspondents gathered to watch the early-morning workouts on the track when the Lochsong Monster, as she had been dubbed, did something that was considered impossible when Dettori let her off the leash.

With his instinctive inclination to perform, Dettori clearly loved the razzmattazz that accompanied every aspect of the Breeders' Cup, not just on the big day, but before it as well. Wearing a maroon and pink jacket, white cap and jeans, Dettori sat jauntily astride Lochsong as the pair were led on to the track by the ample figure of Marilyn 'Fi Fi' Montavon on her pony, Downstream, with Dettori grinning from ear to ear as if he had just won the Kentucky Derby.

What followed that happy little scene became headline news in sports pages from Louisville to Newmarket. When Dettori let Lochsong have her head she sped round the home turn, covering three furlongs in an astonishing 33.1

seconds. Eyes were on stalks and hard-bitten pressmen took extra swigs of coffee to make sure they were properly awake.

Frank Rak of the *Boston Globe*, a colourful character who always has a memorable comment to make, said: 'I thought my watch was broke. I've never seen this in my life. No one on earth has ever seen a time like this. She went from the three-eighths pole to the quarter furlong marker all on the bend in less than eleven seconds and she did it all by herself.'

From that moment Lochsong had a new nickname: she became known as the Louisville Express by the locals. But beneath the euphoria there were several shrewd observers prepared to say that she had ruined whatever chance she had in the Sprint, because by going so fast so close to the race she had peaked too soon.

The British contingent shrugged off such nonsense. Lochsong was a freak, they said; the local horses might as well stay in their boxes. But the nagging worry had become a serious concern by the time Lochsong was loaded into the stalls and the doubters were proved devastatingly correct as Lochsong's swansong became a dirge.

Uncharacteristically slow out of the gate, Lochsong was never able to take the lead let alone dominate. Having turned for home in sixth place with nothing more to give, she fell further and further back through the field in the straight. As Dettori eased off on her, she finished plum last of the fourteen runners.

A desolate Dettori said: 'I never felt comfortable on her. She was concentrating too much on going fast and didn't get round the turn. I felt, to be realistic, that she had a very difficult task. But if you don't take Lochsong who do you wait for – an aeroplane?'

Lochsong came back after the race with a swollen off-fore leg, which partly explained her poor performance but not completely, as Balding now concedes.

'She came back with a slight chip in her knee. I think she must have done it in the gallop,' says Balding. 'I should never have let her work before the race. I said to Frankie "Let her go three furlongs". I didn't realise she had gone so fast.'

In the end it did not matter what the reason was – enough was enough. Smith announced that she would be retired to his Littleton Stud forthwith, and after four seasons of the most spectacular endeavour for her connections and her public, who could deny she had earned the right to bow out with dignity?

Balding staged a farewell day for Lochsong in December, and Emma Balding recalls: 'Frankie sat on her bareback at the farewell day. She gave a buck and he leant forward, didn't touch the reins and stayed on. He's such a good horseman.'

Smith was not quite so phlegmatic about it. 'Frankie frightened the life out of me when he sat bareback on Lochsong,' he said. 'It wasn't planned at all.'

Circus act apart, it was a particularly poignant moment for Dettori, who had just returned from a holiday in the Bahamas, but as ever he made it into a joyful occasion.

'It's the first time I've sat on a horse since the Breeders' Cup – and what a horse,' he said. 'Let's hope her babies run as fast as her. It will probably take

The Louisville Express pulls out: Dettori takes Lochsong for a morning workout on the track before the Breeders' Cup Sprint at Churchill Downs. She amazed observers with an incredibly fast time for three furlongs, but flopped badly in the race.

them three months to catch the foal!'

Memories of her shimmering brilliance will take a long time to fade. Balding recalls: 'When Frankie came into the paddock before the Palace House Stakes in 1995 to ride Blue Siren, he said "I only realise just how good she was now I'm riding some of these others. Blue Siren is good, but Lochsong was a monster".'

As for Balding himself, he admits that Lochsong's departure left a hole that may never be filled. He once said that he had been more fond of her than anything he had ever had, and, looking back, he summarises his feelings by saying: 'Life was so full of interest with her around. Even if she wasn't racing, she was always doing something to make you hold your breath. Life is somewhat duller without her.'

OPPOSITE Farewell my lovely: The Lochsong team (left to right) Dettori, Jeff Smith, Chris Scudder, Ian Balding and Ron Sheather with their heroine on her farewell day at Balding's yard in December 1994. And (right) Dettori, looking tanned after a holiday, sits bareback on Lochsong before a final goodbye.

That last piece of masterly understatement is in direct contrast to the way in which Balding had waxed lyrical about Lochsong in the interview prior to the King's Stand Stakes of 1994. Attempting to encapsulate the qualities that made Lochsong a mare in a million, he quoted from a book entitled *The Look of Eagles* by John Taintor Foote.

The passage read as follows: 'About the head of a truly great horse there is an air of freedom unconquerable. The eyes seem to look on heights beyond our gaze. It is the look of the spirit that can soar. It is not confined to horses; even in his pictures you can see it in the eyes of Bonaparte. It is the birthright of eagles.'

It would surely not be going over the top to suggest that at least part of that eulogy could be applied to Dettori, too.

CHAPTER SIX
A MAN FOR ALL SEASONS

Much is made of the camaraderie among the jockeys in the weighing room, but once on the track it is every man for himself. And at the start of 1994 it was Dettori's willingness to resort to a little dirt – of the strictly legitimate kind – that helped him run clean away with the jockeys' title.

All-weather racing, carried out on a more scientific version of the dirt surfaces that have always been used in America, was originally brought in to Britain to compensate for the abandonments caused by bad weather during the winter. The number of all-weather meetings grew rapidly, and with most of the major players – though not all – looking down their noses at an area of the sport that was considered on a par with non-league football, all-weather racing also came to be regarded as an opportunity for racing professionals lower down the scale to shore up their bank balances.

With his mind set firmly on the title as he moved into 1994 as Sheikh Mohammed's number one, Dettori saw it as a springboard to something far more significant. He had ridden at Britain's first all-weather meeting at Lingfield in October 1989, when Richard Fox, the irrepressible Irish jockey, came up with the memorable quote: 'I've been getting sand kicked in my face all my life, but at least now I'm getting paid for it!'

Little did Dettori realise that he would receive the most handsome payoff of all when he came back flecked with dirt on that historic afternoon at leafy Lingfield. He had ridden at Lingfield and Southwell, the two all-weather venues, during the three winters prior to 1994, but not in a serious way and his total number of rides on the artificial surface during that period was only ninety-three. Suddenly the opportunity to work a little alchemy on the all-weather presented itself and the jockeys' championship would never be quite the same again.

It all happened because of an unlikely benefactor in the guise of a firm of bookmakers, who stepped in to hand Dettori an instant pathway to the crown. The jockeys' title, and for that matter the owners' and trainers' too, had always been decided on the turf circuit, beginning with the Lincoln Handicap meeting at Doncaster at the end of March and ending back there for the November

Handicap (although a minor meeting at Folkestone two days later is the final turf fixture nowadays).

The seeds of change were sown towards the end of 1993 when Kevin Darley had his nose in front of Dettori as they battled for second place behind Pat Eddery in the title race. Darley declared that as he had a licence to ride for twelve months of the year he would do just that and try to whittle away Eddery's lead by riding on the all-weather tracks. Eddery responded by saying that he would do likewise if his crown was threatened, but Darley broke his collarbone so the issue became academic.

With betting on the championship thrown into confusion by this development, William Hill, one of the 'big three' firms of credit bookmakers, approached the Jockeys' Association to ask for guidelines as to the parameters of the championship. After consultations and an agreement by Hills to sponsor the jockeys' championship, it was announced that from the start of 1994 the title period would run from 1 January to 31 December.

Michael Caulfield, Secretary of the Jockeys' Association, says: 'People were under a misconception. Bookmakers can run a book on whatever period they like for the championship, but ever since the introduction of all-weather racing in 1989 the championship had run for the full twelve months.'

Although there were the inevitable reactionary mumbles, no one appeared particularly moved by this development. Most people assumed that the extra period of all-weather would have little, if any, effect on the title because the top jockeys would simply not bother to ride beyond the old turf season. How wrong they were.

An announcement by Dettori on 29 December 1993 that he would be back in action on New Year's Eve, following a holiday, still raised few eyebrows, initially at least. People were clearly still suffering from the excesses of Christmas, most notably the bookmakers, who were caught out by a move that not only hit them squarely in the balance sheet, but also signalled the beginning of a championship-winning ploy by Dettori.

Bets suddenly began to pour in for the Italian to win the title. Having been 9–2 third favourite behind Eddery and Michael Roberts, his odds were down to even money after he rode doubles at Lingfield on New Year's Eve and 1 January. The bookies had seen the light, but for once not fast enough, and several shrewd backers – who presumably had the benefit of inside knowledge – made a killing.

'People got on big time, there was a flood of cash,' David Hood, of Hills, recalls. 'We had to cut Frankie to evens when it became obvious that because of his quickfire start on the all-weather it was going to be a one-horse race.'

Dettori was quick to deny that he had deliberately attempted to steal a march on Eddery and Roberts, but you could not help thinking of Christine Keeler's famous remark: 'He would say that, wouldn't he?'.

Dettori explained: 'I'm not really trying to get a head start. I want to ride from the beginning to the end of the season. I feel fresh, fit and ready to go. I feel great for my holiday. I walked along the beach and was in bed by nine o'clock every night.'

Matty Cowing, Dettori's agent, also insists there was no deliberate jumping of the gun: 'It was not in his mind to steal a lead at all. Frankie just loves riding and he decided to ride twelve months of the year.'

However, at the time of Dettori's announcement Cowing had put it rather differently: 'Frankie badly wants to win the championship and we'll be riding everywhere we can to do it,' he said. 'We're committed to the all-weather and we'll ride through the year.'

There is no doubt that Cowing played a major part in Dettori's title romp, even though the Sheikh Mohammed contract was the key component in his triumph. A good agent, with his finger on the pulse, can make the difference between winning and losing a championship, as was the case with Michael Roberts and the industrious Graham Rock two years previously.

The genial Cowing had always been a racing fanatic, but he slipped into the role of agent as a result of a serious illness. 'I was a factory worker on the machines, but I had a stroke in 1987,' Cowing explains. 'I had lived in Newmarket all my life and I knew Bruce Raymond well. After I had my stroke he asked me to come and work for him as his agent, so I did.

'Then Frankie approached me and said "Bruce says you must take me on". I knocked him back the first time, but he kept saying to me "You must take me, you must take me". We've been together since 1989. Frankie's such a great guy. Because I'm twice his age we're like father and son.'

Cowing was quickly earning his percentage in 1994. A spate of doubles, trebles and a four-timer took Dettori to twenty-one by the end of January, one more than the number by which he had trailed Pat Eddery at the end of 1993.

Dettori's two victories on a moderate animal called No Submission at Southwell moved the horse's trainer, David Chapman, to say: 'I used to think jockeys were only good because they rode good horses.'

Chapman, a veteran of more than thirty years' training, expands on his admiration for Dettori by saying: 'No Submission used to get left in the stalls, but Frankie nearly always managed to get him away well. Horses seem to run well for him. Even when he's sat still he seems to squeeze them and they run for him without a lot of effort.

'Some of these jockeys think they're tin gods, but Frankie's so down-to-earth. He was prepared to get off his backside and come to Southwell in the winter, whereas some of them thought they were too good for it.'

Dettori's total at the end of February had risen to forty-three. When he hit the fifty mark a week later, bookmakers priced him at 7–1 to beat Sir Gordon Richards's all-time record of 269 winners set in the 1947 season. Pat Eddery

Yorkshire trainer David Chapman, who said 'I used to think jockeys were only good because they rode good horses' after Dettori won for him on No Submission at Southwell in 1994.

had come closest when he rode 209 in 1990; but, like Sir Gordon, he did not have his figure boosted by all-weather racing.

By the time the turf season started at the end of March and a sun-bronzed Eddery returned to action at Doncaster, he was ready to concede that any thoughts of chasing an eleventh title to equal his old rival, Lester Piggott, were now unrealistic. The championship was Dettori's bar a mishap.

'Frankie's virtually got it in the bag,' Eddery said. 'But all-year racing is something you've got to accept, we're into a new era now. If I was twenty-one I'd ride on the all-weather like Frankie, but I'm not, I'm forty-two. But I'm not giving up without a fight.'

Even though Dettori knew the title was almost certainly his in all but name, he still had one particular burning ambition to fulfil besides just proving himself numerically superior to the rest. He wanted quality as well as quantity, and although the Sheikh's vast array of blue-blooded horses promised both in

No Pat answer: Dettori (right) with Pat Eddery, the ten-times champion whose crown he took in 1994 when he rode 233 winners.

abundance, winning the races that mattered was something he knew could prove as elusive as a rainstorm in the desert.

The five British classic races – the 1,000 Guineas, 2,000 Guineas, Derby, Oaks and St Leger – are the ones that set the seal on a top professional's career. They are, if you like, the grand slam events of horse racing and without one of those five majors to his name Dettori felt like a Premier League soccer player without a League Championship or FA Cup winner's medal, or a leading tennis player who has never won Wimbledon or the US, Australian or French Open.

After the season's first two classics had come and gone, Dettori might have believed that he was destined never to win one. It wasn't just that he finished second in both the 1,000 and the 2,000 Guineas, but the manner of those two defeats which were both so cruel that he could have been forgiven for emulating television's manic hotelier, Basil Fawlty, and banging his head repeatedly on the weighing room steps.

In the 1,000 Guineas Dettori rode the filly Balanchine, who was one of the fifty horses Sheikh Mohammed had removed from British trainers the previous year and sent to winter in Dubai at his Al Quoz stables on the edge of the desert where they enjoyed the benefits of a perfect climate. The Sheikh likes to oversee his horses first-hand and having fifty of the best under the care of his trainer, Hilal Ibrahim, in Dubai offered him the chance to observe their progress and plan their campaigns personally.

The Sheikh's experiment had been launched in 1993 when Dettori rode the filly Dayflower into fifth place in the 1,000 Guineas. Asked if he would be sending more horses from Dubai to race in Europe, the Sheikh replied imperiously 'Do you think I give up?'. As far as British trainers were concerned, his words were to prove a chilling harbinger of things to come, as we shall see in greater detail in a later chapter.

Dettori had been out to Dubai in April, three weeks before the 1,000 Guineas, to ride Balanchine in a gallop at Nad El Sheba racecourse. Ray Cochrane flew out with him to ride the Sheikh's 2,000 Guineas hope, State Performer, and recalls: 'Balanchine didn't sparkle that day in Dubai and Frankie turned to me after the gallop and said "Ray, that State Performer is a good horse".'

Balanchine sparkled in the classic race, and had she had a nose that was a couple of millimetres longer she would have won. After Dettori on Balanchine and John Reid on Las Meninas had flashed past the post inseparable to the naked eye, and very nearly to the camera as well, connections of both fillies had to endure a seventeen minute wait before the result of the photo-finish was announced and a steward's inquiry into the bargain.

After Las Meninas had been called the winner by the shortest of nostrils, tears of joy streamed down the face of Tommy Stack, her trainer. Stack, the man who will always be remembered for riding Red Rum to his third Grand National triumph, was gaining his first classic win as a trainer. As he accepted the congratulations of Robert Sangster, the owner of Las Meninas, and it seemed the whole of the racing world as well, Dettori was having to come to terms with the fact that expensive nose jobs are not the preserve only of plastic surgeons.

That fact was rammed home two days later when, unbelievably, Dettori was beaten a similar distance in the 2,000 Guineas. Riding Grand Lodge, the deposed ante-post favourite, Dettori looked sure to cut down Mister Baileys as he came with a storming late run, but the Yorkshire-trained colt just held on to

Nosed out: Dettori on Balanchine (nearside) is beaten a nostril by Las Meninas in the 1,000 Guineas at Newmarket in 1994 and, riding Grand Lodge (opposite, whip raised), is beaten the same distance by Mister Baileys in the 2,000 Guineas two days later.

give Mark Johnston and Jason Weaver their first classic success. Cochrane, incidentally, finished fourth on State Performer.

Two more strides and Dettori would have done it. Gutted was the word that sprung to mind, although that seemed inadequate to sum up the pain that Dettori surely had to be feeling. Amazingly though, he took it with extraordinary good grace. He and Weaver had both worked for Cumani and had become firm friends and a few strides past the post a beaming Dettori leant across and gave Weaver a huge slap on the back.

Weaver, who was to prove a persistent, and at one point serious, threat to Dettori's title aspirations that season, remembers the moment vividly: 'Frankie called out "Well done matey, you've won it".'

Dettori, who was genuinely delighted for his friend, revealed that they had discussed the race beforehand. Talking to Jim McGraph on Racing World's video review of the year, he said: 'What a great race it was. Me and Jason talked about it in the morning. We were drawn high and we thought that was bad. But we made our own race. It was me and him battling from three furlongs out to the line.'

Weaver expounds on his friendship with Dettori by saying: 'We feel well-relaxed with each other. Whenever we're together we're laughing and joking and there is continuous ribbing. If I rang him up and asked for a favour he would do it with no hesitation and I would do the same for him. We talk about horses most of the time, we're horse orientated. We enjoy the rivalry, that's for sure.'

Fate had not finished twisting the knife, incidentally. The day after the 2,000

Guineas Dettori finished second on Blinding Speed in the Italian equivalent in Rome. It could only get better, he hoped – and it did.

Looking back, Dettori described his defeat on Balanchine by saying: 'In a way it was bad luck and good luck. That day I realised Balanchine was a staying filly. It hurt, but I realised I had a real good horse in my hands.'

How right he was. Lochsong was incomparable and irreplaceable, but just over a month after the Guineas Balanchine became the other leading lady in his life when she carried him to victory in the Oaks. It was a wet and thoroughly miserable afternoon for the second fillies' classic, but Dettori's winning smile illuminated the gloom like a dazzling ray of Italian sunshine.

Having endured a disappointing run in the Derby on the third favourite, Linney Head, who finished only tenth behind Erhaab, Dettori went to post aboard Balanchine for the Oaks three days later wondering whether yet another classic ride would end in anti-climax.

Racing down into Tattenham Corner his hopes were beginning to rise as he moved up to dispute the lead. But Hawajiss and Wind In Her Hair were going just as well , and when Frankie went to kick Balanchine clear the response was hardly electric.

Instant acceleration was never Balanchine's trump card, although she certainly had pace or she would never have been able to get so close to winning the 1,000 Guineas. She was to prove herself a champion by relentlessly grinding her rivals into the ground. That was exactly what she did that day at Epsom, pulling steadily away as her rivals gradually cracked and eventually passing the post with two and a half lengths to spare over Wind In Her Hair.

Epsom was a sea of brightly coloured umbrellas as the rain continued to tip down, but Dettori wouldn't have cared if it had been a Siberian snowstorm – he had finally put his name on the classics roll of honour and it felt so good. Maybe he had a bit of a way to go to catch up with Old Man Lester, but he was on his way.

As he was pulling Balanchine up after the post, Dettori's emotions took over. He gave a clenched-fist salute and a loud yell of delight. 'That was for my parents, who have been so supportive,' he said. 'I spoke to my father and John Gosden this morning and they said be positive. I was a little bit sour after the Guineas, but this makes up for everything.

'She was very tough and from three furlongs out she galloped them into the ground. After I'd been beaten in both Guineas I was afraid something would come and do me and I kept shouting for the post to come. I just recall the last fifty yards when I felt this ball of energy coming through my body because I knew that I had made it. It was great – my first classic. At the time it was the greatest moment of my life.'

But the best was still to come, and very shortly too. Three weeks later Dettori rode Balanchine to a stunning victory over the colts in the Irish Derby at the

Singing in the rain: Dettori urges Balanchine home to win the Oaks at a rain-soaked Epsom in June 1994, recording his first British classic success.

Curragh. King's Theatre and Colonel Collins, who had finished second and third to Erhaab in the Epsom Derby, filled the places again, but at a more respectful distance. Balanchine simply destroyed them.

Before the Derby, Erhaab's owner, Sheikh Hamdan al Maktoum, had been quoted as saying: 'There are only 25,000 words in English, but there are a million words in Arabic.' Dettori used one special word to sum up Balanchine's performance, a word that he also applied to the other great love of his professional life, Lochsong.

'That day she was a monster,' he said. 'I knew at the furlong pole it would take a machine to pass us, we were going so fast. She annihilated the best of her generation. It was the ultimate performance by a racehorse. No words can describe her – she is unbelievable.'

As Dettori returned to unsaddle, he managed to achieve something that few people, if any, had been able to achieve. The bearded Sheikh Mohammed, who is Crown Prince of Dubai and Minister of Defence for the United Arab Emirates, had always adopted a slightly forbidding, unsmiling presence in public, but on this very special afternoon the young Italian had the Sheikh grinning like a schoolboy who has just been handed the keys to the tuck shop.

Dettori leant down from the saddle to put his arms round the Sheikh, who in turn clasped Dettori's hand and lifted it high like a referee holding up a victorious boxer's arm at the end of a contest. It was the first manifestation of what was to be a continuing public display of affection between the two men. Once again Dettori had demonstrated his ability to bridge all social divides and cultures with his spontaneous enthusiasm.

After her swaggering victory in Ireland, Balanchine appeared to have Europe's premier middle-distance events at her mercy. But racing is a continual

In at the deep end: Balanchine prepares for her successful assault on the British classics with a session in the pool in Dubai in January 1994. She returned there to recuperate from a life-threatening illness later in the year.

tightrope between triumph and disaster, and three weeks after her Curragh victory Balanchine was struck down by a serious attack of colic that put her life in danger. She underwent an operation to remove an obstruction from her small intestine and for several days the racing world feared the worst.

Dettori was stunned. 'It's very sad. I hope she can survive and have babies,' he said. 'She's the best I've ridden.'

Despite a recurrence of the problem shortly afterwards, Balanchine pulled through, but there was no question of her racing again that season and she went to Dubai to recover and be prepared for a four-year-old career.

Simon Crisford, who manages Sheikh Mohammed's Dubai racing operation, says: 'Frankie had such a close relationship with Balanchine, he was in love with the filly. He liked to see her when he came to Dubai and he rode her as much as possible on and off the track.'

Talking of the charisma that so captivated the Sheikh, Crisford says: 'Frankie has such a fabulous personality, he's a star in the broadest sense of the word. He has such style and character that he endears himself to everybody. And, off the track, you couldn't wish to meet a nicer guy.'

There was no Mr Nice Guy when it came to the title, however. Dettori wanted it and he wanted it badly. But, as he began to pile the pressure on his rivals he made what appeared to be an extraordinary announcement at the beginning of June. Weaver, who had been virtually an unknown at the beginning of the season, was refusing to lie down and die at that stage and was only nine behind when Dettori revealed that he was to risk his title chance by taking up a three-month riding deal in Hong Kong.

In a significant turnabout, Dettori had been invited by the Hong Kong Jockey Club, along with Walter Swinburn and Alan Munro. Philip Johnston, the Director of Racing there, said: 'When we refused Frankie Dettori a licence last year we said it was only for that season. He is a very fine young rider and we will probably be welcoming him here as British champion jockey.'

Johnston's last statement seemed a bit premature, to say the least. Dettori's contract was to run from the end of November and would therefore give Weaver time to cut back the deficit on the all-weather if he was still reasonably close behind when Dettori departed.

Whether it was the lure of the dollar that had addled Dettori's mind once again nobody knew, but the bookmakers immediately realised the significance of Dettori's plan and, having been 50–1 at the start of the season, Weaver's title odds were cut from 9–2 to 5–2, with Dettori still odds-on favourite.

Perhaps Dettori felt he could burn off Weaver's challenge by the time he left for Hong Kong, and he was certainly looking good to do just that when he recorded the fastest century ever aboard Winter Coat at York on 11 June, five days after his announcement. Sir Gordon Richards had set the previous fastest on 17 June 1949, but he had not started the season until 17 March and did not have the benefit of all-weather or evening meetings.

It was Dettori's fourth century and as the winners continued to flow he had opened up a sizeable gap on Weaver at the end of June, leading his rival by 127 to 99. There were thirty-five more winners in July, including four at Glorious Goodwood, where he won the Ritz Club Trophy, awarded to the meeting's leading rider, for the first time. Dettori, Pat Eddery and Walter Swinburn all rode four winners, but Dettori took the trophy by virtue of his seven seconds.

It was a Goodwood fixture marred by an unusual series of falls by riders, with Michael Kinane, Jimmy Quinn, Wendyll Woods and Lester Piggott all taking heavy tumbles. Piggott's was the worst. Horrified racegoers watched the 58-year-old grandfather bouncing like a football off the hard ground after he fell from Coffee 'N Cream.

Piggott's helmet came off in the incident and he was given oxygen, and a neckbrace. He also had his feet taped together as he was stretchered off the track. Like the seemingly indestructible character he is, Piggott was back riding within a week; but his fall and those of the other three were the latest in an unprecedented series of accidents that season.

The appalling low point had come at the beginning of May when Steve 'Samson' Wood was killed at Lingfield Park. Various reasons were put forward for the spate of falls, which totalled seventy-seven by the end of the year, but some experts had no doubt about the cause of the huge increase in the incidence of Flat-race disasters.

The new breed of jockeys like Dettori and Weaver had taken the business of riding winners into a new dimension, but in so doing they had set themselves schedules that were at best exhausting and at worst downright dangerous. Dettori was to set a new British record for the number of mounts in a season when he had his 1,069th race on Pastel, a winner at Hamilton Park at the beginning of September, beating the previous highest set by Michael Roberts when he became champion in 1992.

Dettori was to amass 1,319 rides on his way to the championship, but behind that bare statistic was an endless grind of dawn-to-dusk activity, seven days a week, twelve months of the year. Jockeys were travelling the length and breadth of the country almost every day, flitting back and forth from early-morning workouts at stables to afternoon meetings and then on to evening fixtures.

There was also Sunday racing abroad, in which virtually every top jockey participated. And, with the arrival of Sunday meetings in Britain in 1995, the treadmill became even more relentless. Pat Eddery, with no trace of sour grapes, expressed the opinion that the younger brigade of jockeys were in danger of burning themselves out before they were thirty.

In an article highlighting the dangers of the modern Flat jockey's workload, in the *Sunday Times* in 1994, Weaver told me: 'Pat Eddery said to me recently "I don't know how you can keep this pace up". I replied "I can handle it at the moment because I'm young and very fit". But it is very tiring and I wouldn't expect to keep it up for the next ten years.'

In the same article, plans for a programme of psychological help for jockeys drawn up by Dr Michael Turner, the Jockey Club's medical adviser, were examined. Turner had been looking at jockeys' lifestyles in conjunction with John Anderson, chairman of the National Association of Sports Coaches and fitness adviser to the British Olympic Association.

'Jockeys have one of the most extraordinary lifestyles I have ever encountered in sport, especially with regard to the length of their day,' Anderson said. 'Most people would say it's an impossible way of life. And, in terms of carrying out their professional duties, I would say that if you live the kind of lifestyle jockeys do, fatigue will affect your judgement and skill and ability to do the job and, as a consequence of that, accidents are inevitable.

'I was astonished at the poor level of preparation for such a challenging, demanding and stressful profession,' Anderson continued. 'Their ideas for losing weight, in particular, were unbelievably antiquated and potentially dangerous. For example, sitting in saunas for hours and undergoing massive dehydration. In many cases they were getting on horses hardly able to climb aboard.'

Dr Turner backed Anderson's view, saying: 'Jockeys are the only athletes who have to be at their peak 365 days a year, and in many cases up to six times a day. The lifestyle of the jockey is not something that any other normal human being would accept; putting their life on the line for six or seven days a week.'

Ray Cochrane, who had been through the mill himself, underlined the seriousness of the problem from a jockey's point of view. 'You need a break. Tiredness makes you lose your sharpness and your edge,' he said. 'Sometimes you're just going through the motions.

'Frankie Dettori is certain to be exhausted after this season and I remember Steve Cauthen saying to me, after notching up a big score not long before he quit, "I've never been so tired in my life and in the end who cared? I've had enough. I'm killing myself and for what?".'

It was something Dettori alluded to at the end of his 1994 *tour de force*, as we shall see later. But he and Weaver had a crown to battle for and there was to be no quarter given and no letting up. Quantity rather than quality of mounts was the watchword for Dettori in the later part of the season, with Lochsong providing the cream and a facile success on Halling in the Cambridgeshire also spicing up the numbers game.

Dettori reached the 200 mark for the first time when he won on Shoaq Albarr at York at the beginning of September. In doing so, he became only the sixth rider to record a double century in Britain, and as he returned to the winner's circle in the colours of Sheikh Mohammed's younger brother, Sheikh

Ahmed al Maktoum, he showed us a new gesture in his repertoire, a Churchillian V-sign.

Dettori had reached the 200 winners faster than Michael Roberts and Pat Eddery. He was keen to beat his father's post-war European record score of 227, set in 1983, and Sir Gordon Richards's all-time best of 269 also appeared to be his for the taking, especially as he announced he was considering delaying his Hong Kong contract. He gave up the idea of going to Hong Kong altogether six weeks later, saying: 'I'm ready for a break after thirteen hundred rides and I want to defend my title again.'

But, Sir Gordon's record was not in danger. Dettori had already stated as much just before he reached the double century. 'I think that record belongs to Sir Gordon Richards, who was a great jockey,' Dettori said. 'I would consider it an honour to get anywhere near it before I leave for Hong Kong.'

Cowing expands on Dettori's thinking: 'Frankie admires Sir Gordon's record. Deep down he might have thought he shouldn't beat it because it was a different ball game in those days. There were no motorways or planes to take them to meetings and there were no all-weather or evening fixtures.'

On the face of it, Dettori did have a hugely unfair advantage over Richards, but to scoff at any new record Dettori might have set just because of the altered parameters in the sport was as ridiculous as saying that today's champion racing drivers are phoneys because they are using faster cars. And anyway, as Cowing points out, if you took away Dettori's all-weather winners he would still have won the title.

John Randall, Britain's foremost expert on horse-racing statistics, came out strongly in favour of Dettori's achievement. Writing in the *Racing Post*, under the headline 'Dettori haul not bogus', Randall said: 'If Dettori does pass Richards's total, let no one be in any doubt that it will be a valid record, recognised by the *Guinness Book of Records*.

'There have been claims that Dettori's potential record is bogus because he has had more winning opportunities than Richards. But that was true of Richards himself when he was breaking Fred Archer's records ... It is futile to denigrate Dettori's feat on the grounds that the season is now much longer than in Richards's day. So what if it is?'

Randall went on to conclude that the reason many would refuse to recognise Dettori's record was because it was one of the sacred cows of the sporting world. 'He [Sir Gordon] was racing's most cherished hero,' Randall said. 'And even now some people get upset at anything that diminishes his stature – like a young Italian upstart threatening his records ... There is nothing sacrosanct about his records and if they go the same way as Fred Archer's, his greatness will not be diminished.'

The arguments were anyway academic. Dettori hung up his boots at the end of the turf season having recorded a total of 233 winners. Weaver plugged on

Whip hand: Dettori enjoys an easy success on Halling in the 1994 Cambridgeshire
Handicap at Newmarket as he races on towards his first championship.

and reached 200 when he won on Magna Carta at the newest all-weather
venue, Wolverhampton, in November. That was his final total and would have
been more than enough to win him the title had it not been for that annoying
buddy of his.

Dettori admitted that his schedule had taken its toll. 'The hardest part was
the last few weeks when all the big races had finished,' he said. 'After the
Champion Stakes I found it hard to get motivated and after one thousand three
hundred rides I really felt it. We can't keep up this pace for twenty years – we're
going to end up hurting ourselves.'

It was all made worthwhile by the reality of his first championship, something
that meant more to him than perhaps anybody realised at the time. 'Frankie is
very ambitious and hungry,' Cowing says, 'and above all he wanted to be
champion jockey in Britain. He says it's the greatest place in the world to ride
and it has the greatest jockeys. He'd like to carry on winning it as long as he can.'

Being the perfectionist he is, Dettori often tended to dwell on the negative aspects of his season. Ian Balding's wife, Emma, recalls how Dettori was berating himself for the ones that got away just as he was about to fulfil his greatest ambition.

'On Arc day we'd come to Paris in separate planes and Frankie got into our taxi with Jeff Smith and Ron Sheather,' Emma says. 'We were talking about the season and Frankie scratched his head and said: "How did I get beaten on Balanchine in the Guineas? I must have been the only man in England who could get beaten on such a good horse."

'He also talked about two minor races, one of them at Bath, in which he felt he shouldn't have been beaten. He was worrying about the little things when he was going to be champion. He was analysing his mistakes instead of going over all his triumphs.'

It was all a lot more positive when Dettori received his title trophy at the Sandown jumping meeting at the beginning of December. He had just returned from a holiday in Morocco and he probably never dreamed he would receive the kind of reception he was accorded.

There was an announcement at the start of the afternoon that the presentation would be made to Dettori after the third race on the card. Racegoers then stood twelve-deep around the winner's enclosure and it was completely jam-packed inside as he stepped up on the podium.

David Hood, whose firm sponsored the award, recalls: 'Frankie has such public appeal that we decided to make it a ceremony. He had dinner with us before racing and met some of our clients. He was with his girlfriend and seemed very relaxed. People kept saying things to him like "I saw you at Pontefract or Warwick" and he always tried to recall the race. He never got impatient with anyone; he's such a tremendous ambassador for the sport.'

Dettori gave a deeply personal insight into how much race riding and the whole amazing championship year meant to him in an interview with Clare Balding for Radio One's 'Five Live' programme in March 1995. 'My number one love is horse racing – it's been my life,' he said. 'My father has been champion jockey and I just sleep, breathe and eat racehorses.

'It's a great thrill to be out there every day. It's the only place in the world where I feel free and I'm doing what I'm supposed to do. God gave me this gift and I'm taking full advantage of it and enjoying it. I don't wish to have anything else in the world, just things to keep the same. That's enough.

'To come close to last year would be impossible,' he reflected. 'There were three moments that were equally as good – my first classic win on Balanchine, winning on Lochsong at Longchamp and the Breeders' Cup. I couldn't split them. If I have one of those moments again it will be a great thrill. To have three of them was unbelievable.'

The two ladies in Dettori's life were very special, but it is a fair bet that if he

Just champion: Dettori enjoys a huge ovation from the crowd at Sandown Park as he receives the trophy for his runaway success in the jockeys' title race.

could have had one of those magic moments over again it would have been that extraordinary afternoon in Kentucky that he referred to. It was the day when, in conjuction with another Italian, an Arab sheikh and a colt bred in Ireland, he flew the flag for Britain in a way that had even the stiffest of upper lips trembling.

CHAPTER SEVEN
BIG BUCKS IN BLUEGRASS COUNTRY

Ten million dollars is a lot of cash in anybody's language, which is why, despite a succession of gut-wrenching failures in the Breeders' Cup, the British kept coming relentlessly across the Atlantic in pursuit of what was looking more and more like an impossible dream.

While the French appeared to have found the business of winning Breeders' Cup races relatively easy, with nine successes in the first ten runnings of the seven-race programme, Britain had managed only two. The annual drubbings for the Brits had reached the stage where there were those who said there was no point in even bothering to tackle the Americans in their own backyard. But those gloom merchants were completely missing the point.

Money aside, the Breeders' Cup represents the ultimate racing challenge. Heightened by the unparalleled ability of the Americans to put on a show, this glittering extravaganza has transcended the narrow confines of the sport and is regarded not just as racing's premier international event, but also as a unique occasion.

So it was that a record number of twenty-seven European raiders, fourteen from France and thirteen from England, put behind them all thoughts of previous wipeouts and jetted off at the beginning of November 1994, intent on hunting down the greenback in the Bluegrass country of Kentucky. Luca Cumani had tried his hand more than once and failed and, being the pragmatist he is, he approached his carefully orchestrated assault with Barathea in the 1994 Breeders' Cup Mile with a realism born out of hard experience.

'You need confidence when you attempt to deliver in this game otherwise you wouldn't be in it,' Cumani says. 'But you know from experience that you'll get beaten more often than you win. You also know that, sooner or later, when things come together, you'll get lucky.'

In the historic setting of Churchill Downs on a balmy autumn afternoon, everything came together for Cumani in a way that engulfed him in a tidal wave of emotion, as indeed it did everyone connected with the horse and the army of British supporters as well. Saturday, 5 November, was the day Cumani lit the fuse, Barathea produced the fireworks and Dettori detonated an explosion of delight.

It's in the breeding: Barathea's breeder and part-owner Gerald Leigh with some of his broodmares, including Brocade (left), the dam of Barathea.

In truth, it did not look too promising for Barathea from any angle as the crowd of over 71,000, the highest in the eleven runnings of the Breeders' Cup, poured in through the gates of Churchill Downs. France had taken the Mile three times, with Last Tycoon and the brilliant dual winner, Miesque, and Ireland had gained a fabulous triumph with Royal Academy ridden by Lester Piggott just days after his comeback. In contrast, Britain had sent over a clutch of outstanding milers, including Selkirk, Zilzal, Warning and Cumani's pair, Second Set and Markofdistinction, and seen them all beaten out of sight.

Furthermore, while Barathea was regarded as a top-class miler, he was one of those infuriating horses who, through no fault of his own, always seemed to miss out on the big occasion. It was especially frustrating as his auspicious beginnings had suggested the sky was the limit.

A son of Robert Sangster's super stallion, Sadler's Wells, who was in turn a son of racing's grand-daddy of them all, Northern Dancer, Barathea was bred by the noted owner–breeder, Gerald Leigh, from his good mare, Brocade, so he had a pedigree that was pure class from top to bottom.

Leigh, who describes Barathea as an outstanding looking foal, is a commercial breeder and he sold three-quarters of the horse to Sheikh Mohammed when he was a yearling. The Sheikh must have thought he had secured himself a potential champion when Barathea won both his starts as a two-year-old, but he was trounced by the brilliant French colt, Zafonic, in the 2,000 Guineas and, though he went on to win the Irish 2,000 Guineas, the rest

125

The shape of things to come: Dettori rides Barathea to victory in the Westley Stakes at Newmarket as a two-year-old in 1992.

of his three- and four-year-old career prior to the Breeders' Cup was, in relative terms, largely disappointing.

After failing to stay the distance of the Derby, in which he looked the possible winner two furlongs from the finish but faded to finish fifth, it was decided that miling was his game. He was involved in the finish of most of the top mile races in Europe, but he seemed destined never to lift the really big prize his consistent efforts merited and he came to Churchill Downs with a career record of only four wins from fifteen starts.

As far as the Breeders' Cup was concerned, there was something far more worrying than Barathea's persistent bad luck or the signposts of history. The problems of sending horses overseas are extremely complex, and many of them react unfavourably to the trip and the strange surroundings. Cumani had been anxious to send Barathea to Kentucky early to give him time to acclimatise, but his plan was almost scuppered by the horse being too laid back for his own good.

'There were logistical problems because the British runners were all going out on the Tuesday and I wanted more time. I wanted to go the weekend before the Breeders' Cup,' Cumani explains. 'I had to fight my way to obtain permission to spend extra money so that Barathea could go early.

'There were also problems with the quarantine arrangements which had been set up for Tuesday morning. But in the end we managed to arrange a different flight and he arrived in the States on Sunday morning. Everything went perfectly, but the horse fell asleep on the plane and cut his chin. It was a bad cut and needed stitching in Kentucky. Luckily the vet acted promptly and there was no infection.'

Keith Ledington, the lad who had looked after Barathea since his two-year-old days, gives a more graphic description of events. The quaintly anachronistic term 'lad' is hardly appropriate for the experienced Ledington, who first came into racing in 1969. He quit the game for a while and spent time driving vans in Cambridge, but the lure of the turf dragged him back and he is eternally grateful that it did. Nine months after he joined Cumani he was given charge of his horse of a lifetime, Barathea.

'I wasn't allowed to go on the plane with Barathea because only so many racing grooms were allowed to go,' says Ledington. 'So Ian Willows, the travelling head lad, and Dick Pope, the flying groom, went with the horse. I flew up from Kentucky to New York and then got a lift to New Jersey to meet Barathea.

'Barathea had a habit of falling asleep when he was flying. I remember that after the Breeders' Cup Mr Cumani told me to be there all the time with him on the plane back to England and not to take my eyes off him. He went to do it again on the way home. I was reading a book and out of the corner of my eye I saw he was buckling, so I shouted at him.

'When he arrived in the States at three o'clock in the morning, Ian and Dick were both gutted and I saw blood all over Barathea's head collar. It didn't look good at all for the race. Doc Chesney, a famous American vet, came and put four staples in the wound and left a hole for it to drain.

'We had to put ointment on it regularly and he wasn't ridden until the Wednesday. He never stopped eating and luckily the wound healed well. If it had gone the other way and become infected it could have ruled him out of the race.'

The incident appeared to have done little to affect Barathea's general well-being. 'Frankie gave him a blowout on the track on Thursday and he had easy exercise on the Friday,' Cumani recalls. 'You could see the horse was in top form and Frankie was in top form too.'

Dettori certainly was in apple-pie order in every sense. He had come to the States as the British champion jockey elect and he was feeling on good terms with himself. He was revelling in the media glare and the whole intoxicating business of the Breeders' Cup. He was instinctively at home in America because, as Carl Evans memorably described him in a tribute to Barathea, he was 'a showman at ease in the land where they are cultivated'.

Dettori the performer and personality, as opposed to Dettori the jockey, had already been cultivated with broader aims in mind in Britain. The fact that he was a young man who was capable of projecting himself beyond the narrow

Taking it easy: Dettori gives Barathea light exercise on the Churchill Downs track before the Breeders' Cup Mile. The colt had suffered a worrying injury on the flight from England, but responded well to treatment.

confines of his sport had caught the imagination of several shrewd managerial types, including Dudley White, who acted as Dettori's promotions manager.

In an article on Dettori by Gary Nutting in the *Sporting Life*, headlined 'The Face of the Nineties', White said: 'When I first came into contact with Frankie I couldn't believe what I was seeing. Here was a young jockey being surrounded by young girls wanting his autograph. That sort of thing doesn't happen to jockeys on a day-to-day basis.

'I would say that by the time he's thirty he will be a household name. He's got something the other jockeys don't have. He's got good looks, charisma, a great personality – the lot.'

Another man who spotted Dettori's potential as a highly marketable commodity was Peter Burrell, whose company handles top names from all sports and is keen to use Frankie for advertising and marketing.

'Frankie's got the best shot at making it big outside racing anyone has ever had,' says Burrell. 'He's got such charisma. You see everyone round the paddock smiling when he walks in. At the moment he's concentrating on his career and he doesn't have much time for other involvements, but when he does the sky's the limit.'

Dettori certainly impressed the people at the BBC when he made two appearances on 'A Question of Sport'. On the second occasion, on St Valentine's Day 1995, he was shown a film compilation and asked if he could remember a particular race with special significance for him.

A BBC spokesman says:'The Question of Sport team had dug out this piece of film of Frankie's father, Gianfranco, winning the Irish 2,000 Guineas on Pampapaul in 1977, beating Lester Piggott on The Minstrel by a short head. Frankie never knew the footage existed, but he recognised it immediately. He was very emotional and quite moved by it.

'The people who work on the programme remember Frankie as a very lively, bubbly character who was very well received. He is very popular and he is considered to add zest to the programme. He will definitely be asked back for further appearances.'

If anyone needed further confirmation of Dettori's pulling power, it came at the Injured Jockeys' Fund summer barbecue in 1995 when various racing items were auctioned. A day out with Dettori, incorporating morning work, breakfast, lunch and going with him to the races, went for £750, over £400 ahead of the next highest outing, dinner with John Francome. To upstage the charismatic

Playing to the fans: Dettori's colourful ways have made him exceptionally popular with the public. Here he shows his touch with the young and the very young.

A bellyful of Frankie: Dettori gets in the swing in Dubai.

former champion jumps jockey, who is now a successful author and broadcaster, is quite a feat.

Dettori's personality also made quite an impression on a certain American lady and her colleagues when he came over to ride in the 1993 Breeders' Cup at Santa Anita in California. Writing in the *Racing Post*, Rodney Masters quoted the office manageress of a car hire firm in Los Angeles, who rented Dettori a car and thought she was talking to the new Al Pacino.

'Dettori was wearing very expensive wrap-around Camel dark glasses, top-of-the-range Armani suit and requested a fast, flashy motor, a Lexus sports convertible,' the manageress said. 'We thought he was an Italian film star over to do a movie in Hollywood. His personality was giving off sparks like a firework. He captivated us all.'

Our Frankie might well have been able to charm the birds from the trees, but even he couldn't persuade Cumani to ditch the big-race king, Michael Kinane, from Barathea for the Breeders' Cup, especially as the Irishman had ridden him in all his previous races that season and was Sheikh Mohammed's jockey for all major-league contenders apart from those trained by John Gosden. It needed something far more telling than mere persuasion on Dettori's part; it needed another slice of the uncanny good fortune that had wafted him through his career like a guardian angel.

'Frankie had been pestering me all along to ride Barathea,' Cumani recalls. 'Every time he was due to run Frankie would get on to me and ask to ride him. I said "It's not up to me, it's up to the management [Sheikh Mohammed and his team]'". But Kinane had taken up a contract in Hong Kong and although he was offered the ride in the Breeders' Cup he couldn't take it. It was another example of Frankie's lucky star. If the Breeders' Cup had been a week earlier, Frankie would not have ridden him.'

So, Dettori was back on Barathea for the first time since riding him in his two winning runs as a juvenile. Perched up on his back in Sheikh Mohammed's maroon and white silks he seemed to exude an inner belief in the horse and himself. As he took Barathea slowly round the parade ring in the shadow of the famous 100-year-old twin spires of Churchill Downs, a landmark as instantly recognisable in its way as the New York skyline, he almost seemed to sense he was riding on a little crest of racing history.

It was difficult to believe that little more than ninety minutes previously, Dettori had seemed as low as it is possible to get after trailing home last in the sprint on his beloved Lochsong. But, although he appeared to have put that débâcle out of his mind and resumed his usual self-possessed demeanour, he was not complacent by any means.

As he exited from the paddock where so many winners of the most famous American race of them all, the Kentucky Derby, had paraded before him, he certainly could not dismiss the potential difficulties of riding Barathea in a race that always needed a vast helping of good luck.

Barathea had run in the Breeders' Cup Mile when it was held at Santa Anita in California the previous year, but forfeited his chance when he ran very wide at the sharp first turn and finished a somewhat unlucky fifth. Gary Stevens, a leading American jockey, had ridden him on that occasion and Cumani blames him for what could have been a disaster.

'It was jockey error the previous year,' Cumani says. 'Barathea missed the break and the jockey tried to make ground too fast. As a consequence he went into the bend too fast and almost came down.'

Jockey error or not, Cumani was taking no chances with Barathea's steering at Churchill Downs. He commissioned Peter Amos, the man in charge of the Newmarket gallops, to build a replica of the bend at the Kentucky track and Amos phoned Churchill Downs to get the exact dimensions. He created the replica bend on a sweeping left-hand gallop on Newmarket Heath known as Lord Derby's Ground and Barathea was taught to go round it as if he was on tramlines.

'We knew how fast they go round the bends in the States, so we had to get Barathea to go flat out,' says Cumani. 'Peter Amos watched the work and said "The speed they went I never thought they'd be able to go round it".'

Ledington recalls: 'Before Frankie rode him in his final gallop, I rode Barathea on Lord Derby's Ground and he was hugging the bend. He changed his legs and leant into it. He went round it so tightly my foot was brushing the rail.'

Barathea might have learnt to race like a greyhound, but when he drew the number one stall at Churchill Downs, right on the inside, it was felt that it could be against him because he might get trapped against the rail and not be able to get clear to deliver his challenge.

Speaking after the race, Dettori totally contradicted this theory. 'Everyone thought the number one draw was against us because we might not have the speed to get out of trouble early on,' he said. 'But he had finished fourth in the July Cup, so he obviously had speed. I was pleased with the draw, it made the difference between winning and losing.'

Perhaps the only real worry for Dettori was the brilliant American horse, Lure, who was going for an unprecedented third straight win in the Mile. Good though Barathea was, he was facing a champion on his own territory and if Lure was anywhere near the form he had shown the previous two years it might be like trying to climb Everest in roller skates, as Jeff Smith put it after Lochsong's defeat.

Despite having drawn the widest stall of all, which in its way was just as worrying as Barathea's inside berth, Lure was odds-on favourite. Another US-trained runner, Megan's Interco, and one of the French invaders, East Of The Moon, were preferred in the betting to Barathea, whose odds of just over 10-1 struck many

Lure wins the Breeders' Cup Mile at Santa Anita in 1993. He had also won the race in 1992 and appeared to represent a major obstacle for Barathea.

British supporters as the best early Christmas present they had ever had.

As the fourteen runners circled behind the starting gate, with the gold and russet-leaved trees which fringed the circuit gently rustling in the autumn breeze, the temperatures had soared into the high sixties. What a contrast to the scene five days earlier when the majority of the British raiding party arrived. Then it had suddenly plunged twenty-five degrees to 40 Fahrenheit and riders were wearing earmuffs as they rode work on the track.

Now the heat was on in every sense, but Dettori was the personification of icy calm as Barathea was eased into his stall and the loading process was systematically completed. As horses strained against the metal frame of the gate and riders waited tensely for that moment of truth when the barriers burst open and the runners hurtle from the gate, young Dettori was as focused as Linford Christie (the one with the lunchbox) before the Olympic 100 metres final.

Just a second or two for a final collecting of thoughts and it was show time. With an explosion of noise and colour, the fourteen contenders sprang into action and sped off on the million-dollar treasure trail with riders jockeying for position as if every inch gained now was worth at least two lengths at the finish.

Inside track: Dettori and Barathea (white star on cap, extreme right) appear to be in danger of being cut off during the early stages of the Mile, but they had a dream run all the way.

There was a moment when Dettori looked as if he might be in trouble, but it was no more than that. Within a couple of hundred yards he had the perfect pitch, tracking the leaders just two lengths or so off the pace, with Barathea hugging the rail just as he had done back on Newmarket Heath. So far, so good.

Down the back stretch and the outsider, Unfinished Symph, was taking them along at a searing pace with another longshot, Dominant Prospect, in second. There had been little change in the order passing halfway and as they approached the final turn with three furlongs to run, Dettori eased Barathea into third place.

Unfinished Symph was still in front and not stopping as they hit the straight, but Dettori still hadn't moved on Barathea. Looking back at the motionless figure of the young Italian crouched low over his mount, many British fans couldn't quite bring themselves to believe he was going so easily – but he was.

A hundred yards into the straight and Dettori could wait no more. If there were any doubts about Barathea being able to turn it on when it mattered they evaporated in the time it takes to say 'Go get 'em'. Dettori asked for and immediately received what he knew Barathea still had left in a very full tank. The response was not so much electric as electrifying as Barathea pulled right away from the pack to scorch past the post in a record time for the Mile of one minute and 34.2 seconds.

Commentator Tom Durkin, the voice of American racing, responded with his usual arresting delivery. 'Here comes Barathea *UNCORKING HIS RUN NOW*,' Durkin intoned. 'It's Barathea who takes the lead mid-stretch and *WITH AN EXPOSIVE RALLY* runs right by them. Unfinished Symph and Johann Quartz are there, but Barathea goes on to a *CLEAR-CUT AND DECISIVE VICTORY*.'

Alex Solis, who rode Johann Quatz into second place, takes up the story. 'My horse broke slow and had to come from the back and come very wide. You need a perfect turn and some good luck to win a race like that. In the stretch I thought I had a chance, but Barathea was gone. He looked very impressive.

'Frankie was on cloud nine. It's a great feeling to win one of those races. I rode with him when he used to come over four or five years earlier and I got to know him well. He's a very good person and a good leader. I'm sure you'll see lots of kids wanting to be like him.'

Gary Stevens, the alleged villain of the previous year, was one of the first to shake Dettori's hand: 'Barathea produced that terrific turn of foot thay always said he had. After the race I congratulated Frankie. He's a great rider and Barathea's a great horse.'

Dettori later recalled that magical moment when he knew the prize was his. 'It was playing on my mind – I was hoping he was going to turn and he turned beautifully and we had a great position,' he said. 'What a feeling – coming into the straight in the Breeders' Cup and I'm the only one on the bridle. I was

No contest: Barathea streaks past his rivals in the straight to win in course record time.

telling myself to wait until the straight and when I asked him to go he delivered straight away. That last furlong when I was in front felt like a mile.'

Cumani remembers the final act of the drama as if it were yesterday. 'I was watching the race through my binoculars, but I was also trying to look at the big screen in the middle of the track. The most enduring memory for me was when the camera angle changed for the last part of the race and Frankie was just coming off the bend still sitting on a tight rein. That's when the hairs on the back of my neck stood up and my spine started tingling.'

A lot of people were experiencing the same sensation. And, as the tingles turned to tears of joy, suddenly it was carnival time, or perhaps that should be circus time. Those of us who had witnessed Lester Piggott's extraordinary win on Royal Academy four years earlier had been fortunate to experience one of the most amazing and emotional moments in sporting history and we doubted if anything could ever match it.

Lester's resurgence from fallen idol to conquering hero at an age when many people have settled for nothing more energetic than a game of bowls was pure theatre, but Dettori's triumph was, in its way, every bit as dramatic and moving. With grown men blubbering like babies, the aftermath of Barathea's success could have been verging on the maudlin, but when Dettori is involved the mere idea of anything less than a joyous romp is an impossibility.

Barathea's victory was many things to many people, but above all else it was the Frankie Dettori Show and, just as he had done with Lochsong in Paris, he took full and glorious advantage. After standing up in his stirrups as he passed the post, he turned to the packed stands and roared his delight, at the same time raising his whip high in the air like a warrior chief clebrating some great victory in battle.

As the applause rolled round the packed enclosures in waves, British fans at the track, and those watching on live telecasts back in the United Kingdom, had no doubt where Dettori stood in their eyes. The Italian was the best there had been since, well, that man Lester Piggott, and he had a bit more natural charm and charisma than the brooding Lester into the bargain.

As a moustachioed outrider in full hunting regalia led Dettori slowly back on Barathea, it was his fellow countryman, Luca Cumani, who felt the first instinctive reaction to Frankie's overwhelming elation. After all, with Dettori's father back in England and Sheikh Mohammed unable to be there because of official duties in Dubai, who better to share his greatest moment with than Cumani. And, being Italian, there was only one way to do it.

'When Frankie walked in he leant down from Barathea, put his arm round me and gave me a kiss,' says Cumani. 'Emotionally the Breeders' Cup was a great time. Obviously Frankie and I had been through a lot together and it meant a lot to me to have him on Barathea.

'Frankie gave Barathea a fantastic ride and the horse got all the luck he deserved. He had been very unlucky in his career, otherwise he would have been the greatest miler of the last decade.'

Cumani also reveals how the idea of that celebrated leap from Barathea's back, projecting himself upwards through the air from the stirrups in the style made famous by Angel Cordero, took root in Dettori's mind: 'Frankie came and rode the last bit of work on Barathea and Only Royale [on whom he later finished fifth in the Breeders' Cup Turf] before they left for Kentucky. I said to him "If you win a Breeders' Cup race will you do a Cordero?" and he replied "No, I might break my leg". When he was being led back in after winning the Mile, he said to me "I'm going to do a Cordero leap". I said "What if you break a leg?" and he answered "Who cares if I break my leg!".'

Dettori carried off the leap with an ease and flamboyance that made it seem like child's play. Someone else trying that particular party piece for the first time might easily have fallen flat on their face. After soaring through the air with his arms held high, he then high-fived Cumani and began hugging just about everyone who was within reach.

He also got a little carried away with his whip, not so much during the race – although if it had been in Britain he would almost certainly have been hauled

Number One: Dettori savours the joy of winning miling's ultimate prize
as he is led back on Barathea.

before the stewards for being a little over-enthusiastic – but after it.

Ian Willows, Cumani's travelling head lad, explains: 'In the States the jockeys throw their whips to the valets. Frankie was just so thrilled that he launched it like a javelin and it went about fifty yards. I don't think he expected it to go that far!'

Willows has seen most things it is possible to see in racing during his nineteen years with Cumani, but like most of the battle-hardened Barathea team, he was reduced to tears by the occasion. 'It was the highpoint of my career,' he says. 'It was the culmination of a few years' effort and it all came right on the day. I was particularly pleased for the horse because he was such a nice person.'

As Barathea's devoted lad, Ledington was if anything closer to the horse and he responded with a show of spontaneous celebration that almost rivalled Dettori's: 'I couldn't see much of the race from where I was, so I listened to the commentary. Then I saw them thundering towards me and by the time Barathea got there I was already jumping up and down. I sent a few pressmen

Let the carnival begin: Dettori and Barathea return to an explosive reception in the Churchill Downs winner's enclosure.

flying as I ran back to greet him.

'The whole thing was extraordinary, it was a knockout. I remember I picked up Gerald Leigh and spun him round in the winner's circle. When I left racing for a while it made me realise how good it is. One moment like the Breeders' Cup makes up for all the bad days.'

Looking back, Leigh gives a considered overview of the occasion that sums up not just the emotion but the professional satisfaction too.

'What I remember first and foremost is Frankie's confidence, first with the horse and then with the draw,' Leigh says. 'I thought there was a danger we might get blocked in, but Frankie was so confident. That is Frankie's strength – he's rarely caught out in the wrong position. He has this extra-sensory feeling of being in the right place.

'Barathea's victory was a moment of explosive excitement. Afterwards, the feeling you got was of a great rapport between owner, trainer, jockey, breeder and horse – a shared experience. The feeling of having a very good horse joins people together and creates a very special bond. Frankie had been with Luca as long as I'd had horses with him. Frankie's Latin and he's warm and his sheer delight added an extra dimension to the win.'

Not everyone was quite so taken with Frankie's frolics, however. In a letter to the *Racing Post*, a Mr D. Baker of London wrote: 'Dettori's yobbish, self-congratulatory antics marred my pleasure at Barathea's win.' Mr Baker appeared to be in a minority of one, because there was a flood of letters to the *Post* taking him to task over his killjoy attitude and asserting that Dettori's flamboyance was like a breath of fresh air in the sport.

With the greatest victory of his young life safely wrapped up and the euphoria still spinning him round like a top, there was one thing Dettori had to do before he could even consider going out on the town to party.

'I was giving Frankie a lift back to the hotel and we stopped off at the back stretch to see the horse and the lads,' Leigh recalls. 'The first thing Frankie did when we got to the barn was to find a phone so he could call his father. He wanted to share his triumph with him.'

The post-race celebrations were in the end a relatively low-key affair and consisted of dinner in a restaurant in Louisville, which Leigh remembers as 'just a very happy occasion, not over the top'. Cumani savoured what he describes as 'a warm glow of satisfaction', while Dettori, as ever trying to inject a little zing into the proceedings, was poking fun at himself.

'Frankie recited a few things that had happened in the race and then he spent most of the evening telling stories against himself,' Leigh says. 'Like the time he rode Casey for me at Catterick and turned to smile for the camera and nearly got pipped on the post.'

After dinner Frankie had one more call to make, this time to see the unsung members of the Barathea team, Ledington, Willows and Pope, at their hotel. He was still up in the clouds and he wanted to relive the magic of that afternoon with them one more time.

'Frankie's a really nice lad,' says Ledington. 'He came into our hotel room in the early hours of the morning to chat to us about the race. He was still over the moon and he wanted to share it with us. That's the sort of guy he is.'

Back in England the headlines were screaming out the news of the victory that had put the pride back on the face of British racing. Typical was the *Racing Post*'s banner headline 'Yes! Barathea just brilliant in the Mile'.

Just before the Breeders' Cup, Cumani had been quoted as saying: 'These are the world championships of horse racing. We must keep coming back ... There is a lot at stake and it is important that the British horses are able to take home some of the dollars.'

Barathea had brought back a suitcaseful. And, as he boarded the plane back to England and prepared for a well-earned life of relative ease at Rathbarry Stud in Ireland, the cynics had to crawl away quietly and look for another avenue for their small-mindedness. Barathea's triumph showed that with careful planning and the right horse it is possible to cross the great divide and win. If you have a jockey like Dettori it makes it a little easier, too.

Perhaps it should be left to Leigh to provide us with the abiding memory of that glorious day, a recollection that gives us all so much to look forward to in the coming years.

'When I was giving Frankie a lift back to the hotel after the race we got stuck in a traffic jam,' Leigh says. 'While we were sitting there I asked him how he saw his career unfolding. "Do you see yourself riding for a long time?" I said.

'Frankie looked at me and replied "I want to go on riding and having days like this till I die".'

CHAPTER EIGHT
THE GODOLPHIN ITALIAN

One of Frankie Dettori's most endearing characteristics is his ability to treat everyone and every event with the same due care and attention. Whether he is partnering one of Sheikh Mohammed's star three-year-olds in the heady ambiance of Royal Ascot or scrubbing home a selling plater on the all-weather at Southwell, Dettori gives his all in the race, and after it as well.

The story of Dettori's first year as champion jockey principally concerns his association with Sheikh Mohammed and his Dubai-based Godolphin team, which swept through the season on an extraordinary magic-carpet ride of international success. However, Dettori's refusal to stand on ceremony saw him begin the year as he had the previous one, getting down and dirty on the all-weather circuit.

With Jason Weaver the only genuine title contender prepared to tackle Dettori on a regular basis at those early meetings in 1995, it seemed certain to be another solo run to the championship. That was indeed how it turned out as the season progressed, but in the early part of the year there were one or two unsettling and uncomfortable moments for Dettori as he set off on another victory march.

The first seeds of discontent were sewn back in the second week of December 1994, when it was announced that the criterion for the jockeys' championship was to be changed from winners to prize money, both on the Flat and over jumps.

Michael Caulfield, Secretary of the Jockeys' Association, whose members had become increasingly concerned about spiralling schedules and the attendant issues of safety and burnout, said the change had been instigated 'because of increasing pressures on jockeys and to encourage riders to look long-term at their careers and concentrate on quality as well as quantity'.

Many observers immediately criticised the new format, mainly because it was felt it would rob the title race of the head-to-head, adversarial edge that only winners can really provide, as well as giving an obvious advantage to riders with high-profile retainers.

To start with it appeared to make little difference to Dettori, who kicked off

Stooping to conquer: Dettori returns after winning on Success Story for the Queen at Lingfield's all-weather meeting. His presence on the all-weather circuit upset some of the lesser riders, who felt he was taking away their bread and butter.

at Southwell on 2 January and said: 'I decided to ride on the all-weather again because I love riding winners. I had a good holiday for five or six weeks and spent a very enjoyable Christmas with my parents.'

Within a month, however, he was adopting an entirely different attitude and threatening to quit the all-weather because he felt confused over the title situation. Speaking at Lingfield at the beginning of February he said: 'I'm in no-man's land. I don't know whether I'm chasing winners or prize money, on the turf or all-weather or both. I have decided to slow down radically. I'll ride about one a week on the all-weather.'

Perhaps his attitude had something to do with an apparent undercurrent of resentment that was building up against him among the lesser lights of the jockeys' ranks. An unnamed jockey was quoted in the *Racing Post* as saying: 'One or two riders have taken umbrage at the champion jockey winning £2,000 sellers on the all-weather when it's their bread and butter.'

Apparently unmoved by this revelation, Dettori changed his tack a week later and announced that he would be back on the all-weather on a regular basis. His decision coincided with the news that the championship was to revert to winners as a result of widespread unhappiness with the prize-money format. The possibility of separate turf and all-weather titles was being mooted for future years.

When Dettori picked up the all-weather thread in February after his brief withdrawal, he was quoted at 2–1 on for the title. Weaver had maintained his early form and led the champion by twenty-seven winners to twenty-six, but few expected Weaver's challenge to last much longer than the toast at breakfast time, as indeed it proved. More worrying for Dettori at that juncture was his nightmare ride on a recalcitrant female named Lawnswood Lady at Southwell the day after his return.

One of Dettori's irons broke as he came out of the stalls, but he still managed to finish the race and beat two home. He said afterwards: 'I just looked up and screamed for help when it happened. It was the most hairy experience I've had this season. I think I will be going to church on Sunday!'

Reg Hollinshead, the trainer of Lawnswood Lady, is renowned for producing top jockeys. Over the years his protégés have included Walter Swinburn, Kevin Darley and Willie Ryan, so he is well-placed to assess Dettori's merits as he recalls the Southwell incident.

'Lawnswood Lady was taking quite a grip with Frankie,' says Hollinshead. 'After the iron broke he kicked his other leg out of the stirrup and rode quite a bit longer than he usually does. He had an extremely uncomfortable ride and said that he didn't find it much fun at all. But he didn't fall off or anything like that and it showed his horsemanship.

'Frankie is a great stylist and he has a tremendous racing brain. He's also very observant and always gets himself in the right position. He's very enthusiastic too. I remember when he rode my thousandth Flat winner at Chester in 1994, a horse called Mad Militant. He was really beaming. He was just as pleased about it as I was.'

Echoing David Chapman's comments in the previous chapter, Hollinshead says that Dettori thoroughly merited the title because of his willingness to work for it: 'Frankie deserves to be champion because he got stuck in when he needn't have done. He said it was better than sitting at home. He's just as enthusiastic when he comes to a Wolverhampton evening meeting as he is when he's riding at a big track. He attacks it with the same enthusiasm.'

Dettori was riding high at an evening venue of a totally different kind in March when he received two awards at the annual Jockeys Awards dinner in London. He had received the award for Flat Jockey of the Year and Personality of the Year in 1993 and he won the Flat award again for 1994 and also took the overall accolade as Jockey of the Year.

Proving once again that there is a serious brain behind the happy-go-lucky exterior, Michael Caulfield praises Dettori for his invaluable contribution to the work of the Jockeys' Association and jockeys' welfare generally.

'Rarely has a man of his youth made such a contribution to Jockeys' Association affairs. It's quite staggering the amount of input he gives you,' says Caulfield. 'At York in 1994 he and Jason Weaver hired a plane especially to come early to our meeting and he also held a meeting in his house at the beginning of 1995 to discuss the prize money versus winners issue, jockeys' weights, and various other matters.

'Frankie thinks a great deal about the sport. He doesn't just turn up at the races and go home again. He has a particular interest in those not doing as well as him. He's very friendly with a lot of the jump jockeys and when one of them was having a bad run he said to me "Hey, give me his number. I want to ring him up". He's a very thoughtful and intelligent young man and he's extremely popular with his fellow jockeys. I can't praise him enough.'

So much for the ill-feeling against Dettori. As stated in an earlier chapter, there will always be jealousy against anyone at the top of their particular sphere. The allegations that Dettori was taking the bread from the mouths of lesser contemporaries were absurd. You would not expect any other leading sportsman to ease off just to benefit those at the bottom of the pile. Taking advantage of every available opportunity to prove you are the best in the business is what makes a champion.

Weaver was certainly making the most of his opportunities in the early weeks of 1995. By the time the turf season began on 23 March he had managed to increase his lead over his friend and rival and was ahead by forty-six to thirty-six; but even he must have known in his heart that he was living on borrowed time.

It's like this, Jason, me old mate: Dettori goes out for another head-to-head with his great friend and rival Jason Weaver, who was his closest pursuer during 1994 and 1995.

When it came to the serious business of the turf racing, Dettori's heavyweight armoury frequently made Weaver's look like a collection of pop guns.

Dettori's most potent weapon for 1995 was not to reveal itself until the turf season was a few weeks old, in Britain at least, although it had come into being during the winter of 1993/94. As we saw earlier, Sheikh Mohammed had begun sending horses from Britain to Dubai for the winter at the end of 1992, and the first sign that his experiment might bear fruit came when Dettori rode Dayflower into fifth place in the 1,000 Guineas in 1993.

The Sheikh's assertion that he most certainly would not give up on the experiment was underlined by the formation of Godolphin Racing, a company owned jointly by Sheikh Mohammed and his older brother, Sheikh Maktoum al Maktoum, the ruler of Dubai. The idea of taking horses to Dubai was primarily to provide them with the benefits of an ideal climate and the best facilities and personnel that the Sheikh's vast reservoir of petro-dollars could buy. But there was another, more personal reason.

The Sheikh has never been an absentee owner leaving everything to the trainer. He is extremely knowledgeable and likes to be involved in all aspects of a horse's career first-hand. It was largely his innate understanding of racehorses that enabled the Godolphin operation to enjoy such fabulous success in 1995.

Clive Brittain, one of the country's leading trainers, tells a story involving the Sheikh that underlines his uncanny oneness with his horses. 'Sheikh Mohammed knows every one of his horses and he has an amazing memory for the face of a horse,' Brittain explains.

'He came to my yard on one occasion to look at some of his horses and spotted a horse named Hadeer, who he had once owned but sold. He said immediately "Isn't that Hadeer?". Considering how many hundreds of horses he has dealings with, and how many chestnuts like Hadeer, I found that extraordinary.'

Sheikh Mohammed's empathy with horses is not surprising when you consider the long-standing Arab involvement with the equine species. Dave Dick, the former jump jockey who has always had a uniquely colourful way with words, once said: 'The Arabs were racing horses when the average Briton was still dressed in a bearskin, covering himself in woad and chasing women into caves with a club.'

The thoroughbred racehorse as we know it today traces back to three Arab stallions, the Godolphin Arabian, the Darley Arabian and the Byerley Turk, who were imported into Britain in the seventeenth and eighteenth centuries. Britain therefore owes the Arabs much, both in terms of the origins of its racing and the way they have underpinned the sport during the eighties and nineties at a time when the recession threatened to cause wholesale casualties.

Sheikh Mohammed reaped the first major dividend from Godolphin when Dettori rode Balanchine to win the Oaks and Irish Derby in 1994. The Sheikh had sent fifty horses to winter at his Al Quoz stables on the edge of the desert the previous winter, and encouraged by Balanchine's triumph he hand-picked another collection of potentially top-class youngsters from the yards of his European trainers at the end of 1994 and transferred them to his Dubai dream factory.

The trainers in question were understandably getting more than a little brassed off at having their best horses whisked away from under their noses, but there was really very little they could do about it. They hardly wanted to bring about a confrontation with their chief benefactor and risk losing the lot, so it was a case of grinning manfully and bearing it.

Aware of the undercurrent of discontent, the Sheikh issued a very public warning to his trainers at the start of the 1995 turf season. Speaking at a press conference in Dubai, he said: 'I am aware of the problems, but I am not trying to bully anybody. My trainers must remember I am the owner. These are my horses and when you own something and see it every day you always appreciate it more.

'I get annoyed when a trainer tells me I should run my horse at Newmarket rather than Longchamp. I know it is just because he wants to be champion trainer. Is it too much to ask that, having put hundreds of horses into a particular stable, I then ask for one or two back now and then?

'I am a horseman and I like to see my horses. I like to make the decisions and I always do what I think is best for the horse. Wintering in Dubai has to be beneficial, but I own more than 500 horses – plenty will be left in Europe.'

The new man at the helm of Sheikh Mohammed's operation was a shy, bearded former policeman named Saeed bin Suroor. He might have been a total mystery to British Racing folk at the beginning of the year, but within a few months his face had become as familiar as that of Henry Cecil, the ten-times champion trainer.

Bin Suroor had begun training in two garages converted into stables and sold his car to feed the handful of horses he owned before Sheikh Mohammed set him up in a desert stable with all mod cons. From such humble beginnings, and with the assistance of the shrewd Jeremy Noseda, a former assistant to leading British trainer John Dunlop, bin Suroor was to take the racing world by storm with an amazing sequence of major international victories the like of which had rarely, if ever, been seen before.

In the spring of 1995, bin Suroor sent Godolphin horses out to win valuable prizes in the United States, Japan, Hong Kong, Italy, Ireland and Britain. There seemed to be no stopping his desert battalion and when he took Sandown's Eclipse Stakes with Halling at the beginning of July he roared through the £1 million prize money mark and led the trainers' championship in Britain by a mile having won only six races compared with the fifty-three of John Dunlop, his nearest pursuer.

Maintaining his 'Lucky Lanfranco' tag, Dettori found he had tapped into

this vein of gold in a big way. The first big European pay-cheque from Godolphin in 1995 came from his victory on Vettori in the Poule d'Essai des Poulains (French 2,000 Guineas) at Longchamp in May in which he rode a peach of a race to hold off Atticus by a short neck.

Dettori, who had taken Longchamp's prestigious Prix Ganay on Pelder a fortnight previously, enjoyed a memorable afternoon because he had earlier won the valuable Prix Lupin on Flemensfirth wearing Sheikh Mohammed's personal maroon and white livery. The dual triumph sent Dettori into a paroxysm of delight and he did something that was pretty eye-opening even by his standards. As he returned to the winner's circle aboard Vettori he gave Sheikh Mohammed a huge smacker of a kiss and the delighted Sheikh hardly batted an eyelid.

A week earlier Dettori had two rides for Sheikh Mohammed at the Newmarket Guineas meeting that were especially significant. He won the relatively low-profile Mayer Parry Stakes on Tamure and finished third in the 1,000 Guineas on Moonshell. He could not have realised it at the time, but at Epsom the following month these two beautifully bred three-year-olds, fathered by the prepotent Sadler's Wells, were to take him for an unbelievable ride on the roller-coaster of racing fortune.

OPPOSITE Arabian dream: Nad Al Sheba racecourse in Dubai, part of Sheikh Mohammed's stunning new racing set-up.

RIGHT My mate Saeed: Dettori with Saeed bin Suroor, the former policeman who became Sheikh Mohammed's trainer for his Godolphin operation in Dubai and brought off an amazing series of big-race triumphs in 1995.

Moonshell had been trained by Henry Cecil as a two-year-old when she won her only race. Her career followed a similar path to Balanchine's in that she was placed in the 1,000 Guineas and went on to win the Oaks. At Epsom, however, there was little confidence behind her in the market and her odds drifted as the professionals lumped on the 1,000 Guineas runner-up, Aqaarid, as if defeat was not even a remote possibility.

Not for the first time the knowing whispers only signposted the way to Carey Street. Aqaarid was never going well on the lightening fast ground and Moonshell could be named the winner a long way from the finish as Dettori sat motionless, biding his time until launching his challenge a quarter of a mile from home.

It had appeared that it was only a question of how far Moonshell would win, but a real danger suddenly presented itself in the shape of Dance A Dream ridden by Walter Swinburn. The two had a brief battle and there was a point when it might have gone either way, but Moonshell's class carried her through and she pulled clear of her rival on the climb to the post.

After Dettori had indulged in his now-familiar antics passing the post, he treated the gallery to a repeat of his Kentucky theatricals, leaping Cordero-style from Moonshell's back. Then, while Saeed bin Suroor as ever maintained a lower profile than a limbo dancer and melted into the background, Dettori hugged Sheikh Mohammed, who responded by lifting him bodily from the ground. On his way back to the weighing room he high-fived John Gosden, his retaining trainer, who seemed as delighted as Frankie was at the success.

'Last year was different because it was the first time, but this was obviously very special too,' Dettori said. 'I scratched my head a little bit because she wasn't working well ten days ago. But we knew she would stay the distance and that is what happened. She outstayed them like Balanchine did last year. I didn't dare look across at Walter and just kept riding. It was an amazing feeling to win it again. That's two British classics for me. Now I'm only twenty-eight behind Lester Piggott!'

Twenty-four hours later Dettori appeared to have eaten away at Piggott's total again when he rode Tamure in the Derby, which was run for the first time on a Saturday in an effort to revive its flagging appeal. No jockey had completed the Oaks–Derby double since Steve Cauthen on Oh So Sharp and Slip Anchor ten years earlier, but Frankie came so close he must have looked at the video recording several times before he really believed he had missed out.

Tamure, who was trained by Gosden, had not raced as a two-year-old, but after winning all three of his races – at Newbury, Newmarket and York – in the spring it was decided to let him take his chance, even though on paper his form

It's a knockout: A jubilant Dettori is led in by Sheikh Maktoum Al Maktoum, the ruler of Dubai, after winning the Oaks for the second year running on Moonshell.

did not match up to that of the leading contenders. However, his record was remarkably similar to that of the 1993 Derby winner, Commander in Chief, whose three victories prior to Epsom had included York's Glasgow Stakes, which Tamure had won.

The favourite was the unbeaten Pennekamp, trained at Chantilly by the phenomenon of the European training ranks, André Fabre – who Henry Cecil referred to tongue-in-cheek as God. Pennekamp had beaten the most hyped horse of recent years, Celtic Swing, in the 2,000 Guineas the previous month and many regarded him as a near certainty to end Sheikh Mohammed's miserable Derby record, which had seen him run fifteen horses over the years and not even get close to the prize he coveted more than anything else.

Sheikh Mohammed and his family were responsible for seven of the fifteen runners in the 1995 Derby, one of them being the once-raced Lammtarra. This colt was trained by bin Suroor and carried the unfamiliar green and white colours of Sheikh Mohammed's 19-year-old Gordonstoun-educated nephew, Saeed bin Maktoum al Maktoum.

Lammtarra had been trained as a two-year-old by Alex Scott, who had been shot dead by an employee the previous September. Scott considered Lammtarra a potential Derby winner from the beginning and, after the horse won his only start at Newbury in August, he placed a bet of £1,000 on the colt at 33–1 for the Epsom classic.

Lammtarra had been ill with a virus during his sojourn in Dubai, but he began to thrive on his transfer to Godolphin's Newmarket yard to where their horses return in the spring to be prepared for Europe's big races. In the fortnight leading up to the Derby he had impressed his big-race jockey, Walter Swinburn, to such an extent that he told Hugh McIlvanney of the *Sunday Times*, after a workout on Newmarket Heath: 'Ignore him at your peril.'

The race was as dramatic as any Derby within living memory, not least because of injuries to three horses caused by a combination of the firm ground and the breakneck pace at which the race was run. Pennekamp injured a leg coming down the hill and trailed home eleventh. Spectrum, winner of the Irish 2,000 Guineas, also finished lame. Daffaq, in the race as pacemaker for the well-fancied Munwar, broke a leg and had to be put down.

It was certainly a race that separated the men from the boys, as Ray Cochrane, who finished sixth on Vettori, recalls. 'It was a very strongly run race. They went flat out from the gate, they were flying,' says Cochrane. 'That's the reason why so many horses who ran well in the Derby failed to show their form next time out. They all had such hard races.'

There was one thing we knew about Tamure, though, whatever else happened he would not fail for stamina. And, just as he had done aboard Moonshell the previous afternoon, Dettori rode the kind of copybook race round the tricky switchback circuit that would have earned him the plaudits of

Lester Piggott, the acknowledged master of Epsom.

As the outsider, Fahal, set a blistering pace, Dettori was never far behind on Tamure. Having collared Fahal a furlong from home and kicked into a clear lead as the rest of the field struggled to answer the calls of their riders, Dettori must have felt he had the prize safely wrapped up.

Had he looked back as he made his challenge and seen Swinburn working away on Lammtarra still several lengths back, he would never have believed the scenario that was about to unfold. A hundred yards from the winning post Dettori had won the Derby, there was no question in his or anybody else's mind. Then, suddenly, a guided missile appeared on the outside and smashed his dreams to pieces.

Responding to Swinburn's frantic urgings, Lammtarra had winged past rival after rival and cut Tamure down no more than twenty-five yards from the line to win in a time that shattered Bustino's twenty-year-old course record by a second. Lammtarra had justified Scott's faith in the most astonishing way and many people were in tears as the colt returned to that hallowed winner's enclosure.

In a way it seemed almost an irrelevance that Ladbrokes, who had laid Scott

that £1,000 bet, eschewed the rule that death cancels all wagers and pledged to send a cheque for £33,000 to his widow, Julia.

Swinburn, who had been a close friend of Scott, had won two previous Derbys on Shergar and Shahrastani, but he was totally overwhelmed by the poignancy of the occasion.

'This is a very emotional moment, the greatest moment of my life,' he said. 'Coming down the hill I said "Please God, please Alex, give me daylight" and it was like Moses and the Red Sea opening up. Okay, I did believe in God beforehand, but I really do now.'

Sheikh Mohammed was ecstatic as he led the winner in. 'Although Lammtarra did not win in my colours, to win the Derby with a horse from Dubai has given me as much pleasure as winning four Derbys,' he said. 'If Alex Scott had been here today it would have given me even more pleasure.'

But what of Dettori? What was going through his mind as he prepared to fly to Newmarket for the evening meeting and relived the worst moment any jockey can suffer, being collared in the shadow of the winning post in the most important Flat race of them all? It had happened in a similar way to young

Ecstasy and agony: Dettori powers to victory on Moonshell in the 1995 Oaks (opposite), but he watches in astonishment as his Derby mount, Tamure, is cut down just before the post by Lammtarra, ridden by Walter Swinburn (above).

Sandy Barclay aboard Connaught in the 1968 Derby when Lester Piggott brought Sir Ivor with a devastating late run to rocket past Barclay in the last hundred yards.

A tearful Barclay had been inconsolable, but Dettori being the kind of positive personality he is took defeat with such good grace that if you had not known his fate you might have thought he had won it. If there was any angst inside he certainly never showed it.

Dettori was obviously feeling the same kind of high as Jason Weaver, who commented after the Derby that just to be involved in those great races, even as an also-ran, was a unique feeling. 'There's something special about being involved in the classics,' Weaver said. 'It's like being part of history as it happens.'

Dettori summarised his defeat by saying: 'I thought I was going to win, but the winner had too much gas close home. I had an unbelievable ride but Wally came there and beat me. Lammtarra must be a great horse.'

Swinburn and Dettori are good friends and travelled to and from Epsom together. Swinburn recalls a fascinating little exchange between them after the two classics: 'After he beat me in the Oaks, Frankie turned to me and said "It's your turn tomorrow". I remember the look of total shock on his face as we were pulling up after the Derby and I told him he was right. I don't think he really believed it would work out quite like that when he said it!'

Anyone who happened to be eating in one of Newmarket's most popular restaurants, The Fountain, that night would not have forgotten it in a hurry. Dettori, Swinburn and many of the Godolphin team including the stable lads were in riotous form, spraying anyone and everyone with champagne and generally whooping it up with no holds barred. No wonder Dettori once said he liked England on a Saturday night because the English really knew how to enjoy themselves.

If there were any thoughts of coming down to earth with a bump it would have happened two days later when he travelled up to Pontefract for what appeared to be the most mundane day's racing. But, far from being a nothing afternoon it turned out to be quite a significant one when Dettori rode Persian Secret to an easy victory to complete a fourth successive century of winners.

The latest hundred had come only a day later than the previous year when he recorded a score of 233 and looked likely to challenge Sir Gordon Richards's all-time best of 269. But as the winners continued to flow there was a subtle but noticeable difference in Dettori's schedule.

The change, although minor, suggested he was taking notice of his own caveat that no one could keep going for too long at the pace he and Weaver had been maintaining. He said as much at Pontefract after he reached the hundred and added a little sop to the bread-and-butter boys as well.

'It's always an achievement to ride a hundred winners and it has been a great season,' Dettori said. 'But I would rather the championship were decided just on the turf season, as it would give the lesser riders more of a chance on the all-weather. Although I enjoy riding tremendously I can't go on like this for another twenty years. But if the others look like catching me I'll continue to ride until the end of the year.'

The practice of travelling on automatically to evening meetings after an afternoon's graft at the track was scaled down and Dettori even took the odd day or two off completely to recharge his batteries. Matty Cowing, his agent, explains: 'I've knocked the evening business on the head. If there's nothing worth riding and no one rings up I'll say we're not doing it. There's no point in sending Frankie there just for the sake of it.'

Needless to say, it took no persuasion whatsoever to motivate Dettori for the most glittering meeting of the year, Royal Ascot, which held out a special promise for him in 1995. With a book of rides over the four days that other jockeys might have killed for, he was installed a firm favourite to win the Ritz Club Trophy. But, not for the first time, he found his way barred by Michael Kinane, who was riding out of his skin.

Kinane wrapped the title up with four winners in the first two days, including a hat-trick on the second day. But Dettori roared back with a magnificent threesome on the third day when Weaver stole a little of his pal's thunder by riding a superb tactical race to lift the Ascot Gold Cup on Double Trigger.

Dettori showed us a little magic of his own when he had the traditionalists among the Ascot crowd cheering wildly as he carried the Queen's colours to victory on Phantom Gold in the Ribblesdale stakes. His consummate artistry on a filly who tended to become overwrought before her races not only gave

Ton-up boy: Dettori gives Persian Secret a grateful pat after recording his fourth successive century at Pontefract in June 1995.

him his initial strike of the meeting, it also provided the first royal victory since Colour Sergeant won the Hunt Cup three years previously. No wonder Dettori was heard to shout 'Alleluia!' when he went out to ride in the next race.

With a hatful of good rides to come on the final afternoon, Dettori was reinstated as odds-on favourite to take his first Ascot title, but neither he nor Kinane added to their score. Dettori was then charged with the bitter-sweet task of receiving the trophy from the Queen on behalf of Kinane, who was riding in Ireland on the Saturday when the ceremony took place, and he carried it off with commendable good humour.

Consolation came swiftly and handsomely. A month later, as Dettori was sailing on towards a second jockeys' title, he achieved something far more important to him than putting on the Ritz (which he achieved when he won the trophy at Glorious Goodwood for the second year running at the end of July). He became an Ascot topper in his own right when he stepped up to receive another trophy from the Queen at Ascot after riding the Derby winner, Lammtarra, to a thrilling win in the King George VI and Queen Elizabeth Diamond Stakes.

The victory of Lammtarra and Dettori was an occasion of pure joy, but the pre-race scenario had been shrouded in controversy. The racing world had been shocked when it was announced four days before the Ascot event that Walter

Swinburn, who had ridden the horse to victory in the Derby, was to be replaced by Dettori.

Not only had Swinburn handled Lammtarra so effectively, he had also ridden a masterly race to win the Eclipse Stakes at Sandown Park on Halling, carrying Godolphin's distinctive peacock blue colours with the Emirates logo, just two weeks before the King George. Dettori, incidentally, had rejected the Eclipse mount on Halling, on whom he had won the 1994 Cambridgeshire, in favour of another Godolphin horse, Red Bishop, who finished third.

Although Dettori was Sheikh Mohammed's retained rider for his horses trained by John Gosden, and the Sheikh also had a second claim on him for the Godolphin horses, many people seemed to feel that 'jocking off' the man who had won the Derby was unbelievably disloyal.

After the race the Sheikh dismissed such notions by saying: 'It is no big deal, it happens all the time in America. We still believe in Swinburn and he will still ride for us.' He then added, cryptically, 'We should not fish in shallow waters. We should go deeper,' and when questioned what that meant he said: 'Don't talk politics in sport.'

There were many theories as to the real reason for the switch, including the suggestion that Swinburn was being disciplined for failing to come up with a good enough excuse for not making it across the Channel to ride two of the

OPPOSITE AND RIGHT By George, I've done it: Dettori achieves one of his most cherished ambitions as he urges the Derby winner Lammtarra ahead of Pentire to win the 1995 King George VI and Queen Elizabeth Diamond Stakes. And he shows his delight as he returns to unsaddle.

Maktoum family's horses in Paris the previous Saturday.

Maybe there was a punitive element in the decision, but the bottom line was that Dettori was the Sheikh's jockey and he had every right to give the ride on Lammtarra to the young man he admired above all others. Lammtarra had still been something of an unknown quantity before the Derby when Dettori had partnered the more experienced Tamure, but when Lammtarra came to Ascot strongly fancied to win the King George, Sheikh Mohammed wanted the best in the business and that could mean only Dettori, whose riding and *joie de vivre* had brought him such pleasure on numerous occasions.

The King George is second in importance only to the Prix de l'Arc de Triomphe in Europe's programme of all-aged middle-distance races. And the field that lined up for the Ascot showpiece in 1995 made it a true championship event. Besides Lammtarra, Sheikh Mohammed's own colours were carried by the 1994 Arc hero, Carnegie, and the 1995 Irish Derby winner, Winged Love, both trained in France by André Fabre.

The one who was expected to show them all a clean pair of racing plates, however, was Pentire, the horse who had come up in relative terms via the backstreets. Pentire, who had never been entered for the Derby, had wiped out all opposition in England in four races that season. And at one point in the King George he looked very much like humbling the best in Europe too.

Tactics are everything in these small but select fields, and with riders watching each other like pursuit cyclists, scrutinising every twitch, it always looked like being a dramatic finale. When the pace-setting Broadway Flyer dropped back as they wheeled round into the straight, Strategic Choice went for home, but he was soon swallowed up as the race resolved itself into a gripping duel between Pentire and Lammtarra in the final furlong.

Oozing confidence, Michael Hills had brought Pentire through from last to first, seemingly to snatch the prize; but no sooner had he edged into the lead than Dettori found Lammtarra answering his every call, demonstating that he had courage to complement his outstanding class and finishing speed. Battling past Pentire in the final hundred yards, with Dettori riding a wonderfully stylish finish without resorting to maximum force, Lammtarra passed the post a neck to the good, thus cocking a sizeable snook at those who said the form of his Derby win was moderate.

Had they gone another hundred yards the margin of victory would have been far greater. Furthermore, the slow pace had not suited Lammtarra and he had also had to recover from a bump which knocked him out of his stride at one point. So when Nigel Gray, the official handicapper, put Lammtarra on a mark that rated him the worst King George winner since classifications began in 1977, the downgrading simply did not make sense to a lot of people.

Dettori obviously thought the horse was Sea Bird, Mill Reef and Nijinsky rolled into one. He was high as a kite and demonstrative even by his standards.

Hills, who congratulated Dettori as they pulled up, recalls: 'Frankie was absolutely chuffed to bits.'

There was much fist-clenching and yet another Cordero leap from Lammtarra in the winner's enclosure to delight the crowd. As Dettori soared through the air, arms held aloft, the thought occurred that the leaps were almost in danger of becoming commonplace and you wondered what he will do for his next trick. Perhaps he might take a leaf out of Sheikh Mohammed's book and gallop past the post standing up Cossack-style on the horse's back, as the Sheikh did to entertain guests at his wedding.

Dettori then enjoyed a typically light-hearted *tête-à-tête* with the Queen as he received his prize, clutching her gloved hand in his two hands in a new little breach of protocol that clearly had the sovereign entranced. Doubtless we will see him inviting her back to tea at his place in Newmarket before too long.

After the royal interlude, Dettori went off to ride in the next race still buzzing with the momentousness of it all. As he walked towards the paddock he jumped up on the back of his good mate, Jason Weaver, out of pure exuberance.

Besides the celebrations there were also debts to acknowledge. Dettori's first thought when talking about the race afterwards had been to thank Swinburn

My father the hero: Frankie with his father Gianfranco at Ascot the day before his success on Lammtarra in the King George. They have remained very close throughout Frankie's career.

for his cooperation. 'I spoke to Walter on Friday and he was very nice about it,' Dettori said. 'He helped me a lot. Without his advice I might not have won.

'Walter told me "Be bold with him and dig deep because he will find more". There were a lot of doubts about Lammtarra, but he showed himself to be a true champion. You find a better horse now!'

Speaking about his rapture at winning the race, Dettori went on: 'A lot of great horses have won the King George. It is one of the best races in the world and winning it is so important to me. It was an unbelievable feeling when I passed the post, it sent shivers up my spine. It was one of the best moments of my life.'

There will be many more such moments to savour, but perhaps we should end this portrait of a remarkable young man by looking back at his triumph for the Queen on Phantom Gold at the Royal Ascot meeting. The horse's trainer, Lord Huntingdon, recalls an amusing postscript to that race which could only have been inspired by Dettori. 'Frankie was obviously elated and he asked permission to kiss the horse. He said to the Queen "Do you mind, ma'am, if I give her a winning kiss?". Princess Anne was standing nearby and she observed dryly "I hope the kissing will stop at the horse!".'

As far as Frankie's ever-growing army of fans is concerned, the kissing should never, ever stop.

Royal smacker: The Queen watches approvingly as Dettori kisses her filly Phantom Gold after winning the Ribblesdale Stakes at Royal Ascot in 1995.

SUMMARY OF
FRANKIE DETTORI'S CAREER

Born Milan, 15 December 1970. Father, Gianfranco Dettori, champion jockey of Italy 13 times.

1985 Joins Luca Cumani as an apprentice, but is too young to ride in races in Britain.

1986 Rides first winner, Rif, at Turin on 16 November, and 16 more in Italy during 1986/87 winter.

1987 Rides first British winner, Lizzy Hare, at Goodwood on 9 June, and finishes season with eight wins.

1988 Rides 22 winners in Britain.

1989 Becomes champion apprentice with 75 wins, equalling Edward Hide's post-war record. Loses apprentice allowance when winning on Versailles Road at Beverley in July. Awarded position as stable jockey to Cumani for 1990 when Ray Cochrane announces he is leaving to join Guy Harwood.

1990 Rides 141 winners and finishes fourth to Pat Eddery in jockeys' table. Gains first Royal Ascot success on Markofdistinction in Queen Anne Stakes and first Group One victory on the same horse in the Queen Elizabeth II Stakes at Ascot. Becomes first teenager to reach a century of winners in a season since Lester Piggott in 1955.

1991 Finishes seventh to Eddery in jockeys' table with 94 wins. Gains first classic win in Europe on Temporal in German Derby. Wins Sussex Stakes at Goodwood on Second Set.

1992 Rides 101 winners and finishes seventh in table behind Michael Roberts. Wins inaugural Young Jockeys' World Championship in Japan. Wins French Derby on Polytain and Ascot Gold Cup on Drum Taps.

1993   Rides 149 winners to finish second to Pat Eddery in championship. Wins Young Jockeys' World Championship for second time. Gives up job with Cumani after offer of lucrative contract to ride in Hong Kong, but forfeits Hong Kong job after being involved in alleged drugs incident. Gains first win on Lochsong and then rides her to victory in the King George Stakes at Goodwood, Nunthorpe Stakes at York and Prix de l'Abbaye de Longchamp. Wins Ascot Gold Cup for second year running on Drum Taps. Secures job as first jockey for Sheikh Mohammed's horses trained by John Gosden.

1994   Rides 233 winners to take first jockeys' title. Wins King's Stand Stakes, King George Stakes and Prix de l'Abbaye, for second time, on Lochsong. Gains first British classic success on Balanchine in the Oaks and then rides her to victory in the Irish Derby. Records fastest ever century when winning on Winter Coat at York in June, beating Sir Gordon Richards's record set forty-five years earlier. Becomes sixth rider to amass 200 winners in a season in Britain when scoring on Shoaq Albarr at York in September. Rides Barathea to win Breeders' Cup Mile in Kentucky for Cumani and Sheikh Mohammed.

1995   Gains fourth successive century of winners. Wins French 2,000 Guineas on Vettori. Gains second Oaks triumph aboard Moonshell. Wins King George VI and Queen Elizabeth Diamond Stakes at Ascot on the Derby winner Lammtarra. Rides Classic Cliche to victory in the St Leger to record 1,000th win in Britain.

CAREER TOTALS IN BRITAIN

1987	8
1988	22
1989	75
1990	141
1991	94
1992	101
1993	149
1994	233